CRACKING THE READING CODE

WITH

THE BRAIN IN MIND

Accessing The Brain's Backdoor
For Reading, Learning, And Teaching

KATIE GARNER, M.Ed.

Illustrations By Daniel Charlson
Edited & Designed By Angela M. Raimondo

Marenem, Inc.
Asheville, North Carolina

Additional copies of this book are available by visiting www.TheSecretStories.com.

ISBN-978-0-692-74536-6

Dedication

For every teacher who has said,

"It just is...

It just does...

You'll just have to remember..."

Foreword

"Beware of the stories you read or tell, as beneath the waters of consciousness, they are altering your world." —*Ben Okri*

Can you breathe underwater?

Of course not, you say. But what if you lived in a world where breathing underwater was commonplace? Then you would say, *yes*! The answer depends on the context.

Similarly, the idea of teaching high-leverage phonics skills to beginning grade level learners, who don't even know all of the individual letters and sounds, would be considered developmentally inappropriate, if not impossible.

Giving the skills, however, is a completely different story! By wrapping skills into stories, the SECRETS "give" learners what can't be easily taught. Stories pose no developmental harm, nor are they grade-specific. Kids simply take away what is personally meaningful and relevant to them without any expectation.

SECRET STORIES® aren't like other stories, as they are rooted in what kids already know and understand—familiar frameworks of social and emotional experience and understanding. And herein lies the power of SECRET STORIES® as a "backdoor" delivery method for the totality of skills that all readers and writers need, but traditionally cannot have—until they are "ready."

So hold your breath and prepare to dive into a new way of thinking about what you can do, and when and how you can do it, as we follow the brain science. In no time, you *and* your students will be breathing underwater!

About Me

Prior to embarking on a teaching career and pursuing a Master's Degree in Elementary Education and Reading, I attended The Juilliard School in New York City, and received a Bachelor's Degree in Voice and Language Studies. Juilliard placed a strong emphasis on the study of languages, including Italian, French, German and English, as well as an understanding of the International Phonetic Alphabet (IPA). This was of tremendous value to me as a singer, but it wasn't until years later, after I began teaching, that it proved even more so.

The concept of thinking outside the box— something that creativity by its very nature demands— was an unwritten requirement at Juilliard. This highly creative learning environment would later serve as the catalyst for the creation of *Secret Stories®*, which provides a context in which learners are bombarded from all directions in a unique and creative way to facilitate easy and effortless phonics skill acquisition. *Secret Stories®* create an optimal learning environment in which students enjoy multiple options and inputs for learning. They consist of varied and simultaneous modalities, or layers of instruction, including: visual icons, auditory and kinesthetic motor skill manipulations, as well as a variety of dramatic and emotive cuing systems designed to target the affective "feeling" domain. This backdoor approach to phonics skill instruction enhances the abilities of *all* learners to make multiple and meaningful connections to newly introduced skill concepts. It is with a dramatic creativity that I aligned traditional phonics skill instruction with current neural research on learning and the brain— specifically how our brains actually learn *best*.

"Miracles become common and consistent when teaching with the brain in mind."

—*Eric Jensen, Brain-Based Learning*

SECRET STORIES® is a brain-based solution to the age-old problem of how to teach meaningless phonics skills in a meaningful way.

It is not a program, but an open-ended, cross-grade level, teaching "tool-kit" for fast-tracking learner-access to phonics skills by providing the logical explanations for letter sound behavior that the brain craves. These logical explanations are shared in the form of "secret" stories, which are the reasons WHY letters make the sounds that they do when they get together in words.

SECRET STORIES® targets phonics skill instruction to earlier-developing, social-emotional learning systems— aligning letter-behavior with kids' own behavior. By connecting abstract phonics skills to already familiar frameworks of learner experience and understanding, they become meaningful and relevant, thereby marking them for memory and prioritized learning in the brain.

Working seamlessly with existing reading curriculum and instruction, SECRET STORIES® accelerates learner-momentum in both reading and writing—breaking down the grade level walls that delay learner-access to the 'whole' code. SECRETS make phonics make sense, and sharing them ensures the early, intensive and expert-level of literacy instruction that's needed to teach ALL kids to read.

SECRET STORIES® is an explicit, systematic and multi-sensory approach to reading and phonics skill instruction that is based on the brain's system for learning,

Contents

1 **Using** *Secret Stories*®— A comprehensive overview for each component of *Secret Stories*®.

- Introduction 13
- *Secret Stories*® Quick Start Guide 19
- Introducing A Secret 23
- Reading And Writing With The Secrets 26
- Body Intelligence 30
- The Posters 32
- The Musical Blending Brain Teasers Download 34
- Secret Skill Sheets 40
- Teachers And Parents 44

2 *Secret Stories*®—Classified— The stories and images that explain the sounds that letters make.

Secret Stories® INDEX

Superhero Vowels® 52	ey / ay 90
Superhero a 54	eu / ew 92
Superhero e 56	qu 94
Superhero i 58	kn / wr / mb / rh / gn 96
Superhero o 60	ce / ci / cy & ge / gi / gy 98
Superhero u 62	ch 100
Mommy e® 64	ph 102
Babysitter Vowels® 66	sh 104
Sneaky y® 68	th 106
i Tries on e for Size 70	wh 108
Two Vowels Go A-walkin' 72	gh 110
ar 74	ing / ang / ong / ung 112
al 76	ed 114
er / ir / ur 78	ion / tion / ation / sion 116
or 80	ion 118
au / aw 82	ie 120
ou / ow 84	ous 122
oi / oy 86	Supersonic Blends 124
oo 88	

3   **Why *SECRET STORIES* Work**— This backdoor approach to the brain is backed by research and science showing how our brains actually learn best.

- The Paradigm Shift 129
- Accepting Exceptions 137
- Outlaws And Word Jail 145
- Evidence Base 153
- Musical Brain Teasers 159

4   ***SECRET STORIES* Handouts And Cut-Apart Cards**— Use these pages with your students.

- Sonic Blends Worksheet 172
- Parent Letter 173
- Word Jail And Outlaw Word Mug Shot Cards 175
- SECRET Skill Sheets 179
- Mini Visuals: Cut-Apart Cards 217

Introduction

Secret Stories® creates a backdoor for learning that accelerates learner access to the code and increases early learner-momentum in both reading and writing. It differs from traditional core reading and phonics programs in that it aligns instruction to work naturally with the brain rather than in opposition to it by making use of more readily accessible, non-conscious learning channels.

Secret Stories® mimics the social and emotional world that children live in and understand, long before their higher level, executive functioning centers have fully developed. Working in alignment with both early literacy and brain development research, *Secret Stories®* targets phonics skill instruction to the earlier developing, social and emotional "feeling" networks (or affective domain) for accelerated skill mastery from the earliest possible grade levels. In this way, *Secret Stories®* provides a much needed base of support for any core reading and/or phonics program. It is intended to both underscore and complement existing curriculum and instruction across the elementary grade levels and beyond, as needed.

Secret Stories® is not a phonics program, as it is designed to work in harmony with existing reading curriculum and instruction. SECRETS are shared in context throughout the instructional day, whenever and wherever they are needed to help students read and spell words.

In this book, you'll find an easy to use reference at the beginning that guides you through preparation for integrating *Secret Stories®* into your classroom, including: day one exercises, the first two weeks, using the Better Alphabet™ Song (in download), hanging the posters, and everything else you need to know as the

NO MORE!

No more having to tell students, "It just is, it just does, you just have to remember." Now you can tell them *why* letters are who they are and say what they do.

NEED TO KNOW

Learners begin to realize quite quickly that:

Anytime a letter in a word isn't doing what they think it should, OR

Anytime they cannot read or spell a word,

There must be a SECRET they have not yet been told!

This will drive them crazy– prompting their need to know more!

TEACHING IN CONTEXT

SECRET STORIES® are systematically shared and revisited throughout the entire instructional day and across all content areas– whenever and wherever they are needed to help kids read and spell words.

year progresses. Also included is information about how to share components of *SECRET STORIES®* with parents and how to best use them at home.

As a teacher, you need only to display the SECRETS around the room and familiarize yourself with the stories (see "Classified" section) and then you can begin slipping the SECRETS into your everyday instruction. *SECRET STORIES®* are meant to be taught in context of ongoing daily instruction, and not sequestered in a designated, instructional block. That isn't how our brains learn best and that's not how *SECRET STORIES®* is designed to work. Take the opportunity to share a SECRET that helps learners decode a tricky word like *August* on the calendar, or *lunch* on the sign where they line up to go to the cafeteria each day. You can also take time when lining up to sing "Beethoven Blends" or "Apples and Bananas" (see musical brain teasers download) so that you can help to increase their level of automaticity with the SECRET you just shared.

Systematically teaching and revisiting SECRETS in context and across the entire instructional day enables learners to quickly acquire critical phonics skills without having to rely on repetitive, skill-based practice, leaving them free to partake in the authentic reading and writing opportunities that occur naturally throughout the instructional day. This allows for natural reinforcement across the entire curriculum, as opposed to confining phonics skill instruction to an isolated reading block or lesson. The result is accelerated access to the *whole* code that learners need to read and write, regardless of grade level.

A great example for how to incorporate *SECRET STORIES®* into daily instruction is to consider your classroom on the very first days of school. Traditionally in an early grade classroom, you may only cover the letter *a* in the first week, and how it sounds short in words like *apple* and long in words like *ape*. But what do you say to the child who sees the word *August* on the calendar and wants to know why that *a* isn't following the rules, and instead sounds like a short *o*? Without knowing the Secrets, you may say something like, "Sometimes, letters just don't follow the rules," or "That's just the way it is," and then send the student away without satisfying their natural curiosity. What a lost opportunity!

This scenario presents the perfect opportunity to share the Secret about *au / aw* and the sounds they make together because they have a crush on one another (*Awwww*, isn't that sweet? *Awwww-gust*). With Secret Stories®, you will be able to answer those dreaded questions about why letters make the sounds that they do! Simply share Secrets whenever and wherever they are needed, so as to meet your students where they are.

The calendar situation described above is a real-life example from my own classroom, where students recognized that the *a* in *August* didn't sound like a short or long *a*. Knowing the Secrets, I was ready to answer their question and said, "I wonder if there is a grown-up Secret that explains why *a* isn't doing what it should?" I could point to the wall, where the *Secret Stories*® posters are hung, and ask if they see any of the same letters that are in the word *August*. When they spot *au / aw* holding hands, they know that there's a Secret. Then I shared that sometimes letters act differently with their friends— just like they may act differently with *their* friends— and I tell them the Secret that explains this new sound. They easily remember this Secret, as it isn't some obscure story about letters, but a story about friendship and behavior, something all children understand on a very base level at the earliest age. Then, when they are ready, they can apply their newfound skills to text.

THE SECRET

These letters have a huge crush on each other and whenever they're together in a word they get so embarrassed that they always say *awwww*, like in the word *August*.

LETTERS ARE LIKE KIDS

Like kids, the letters behave beautifully when separated from one another up on the wall or on an alphabet chart. But when they get close together in words, all bets are off and entirely new sounds emerge!

As fluent readers ourselves, we know and understand that the English language is ripe with letter sound discrepancies. Letters almost never make the sounds that they make by themselves when they come together in real words. So how do we help children to account for all of these apparent contradictions? Simply tell them that there are grown-up SECRETS in the words they can't read and ask if they want to learn them. Do you know any child who doesn't get excited about knowing a grown-up secret? Me either. So from the very first day of instruction, you can help your students begin decoding and understanding text by letting them know they have lots of grown-up reading and writing SECRETS to learn!

Traditional letter sound and phonics instruction, particularly at the primary grade levels, often wants teachers to wait to discuss the sounds letters make until studying those sounds. However, real life reading and writing doesn't work that way. SECRET STORIES® provides teachers an easy way to share them all, but in context, and when learners actually need them. Disguising phonics skills as grown-up reading and writing "secrets" that learners *want* to know, rather than as phonics rules they have to learn, makes them easy to teach at any grade level. Research shows that we learn best when we are curious, and weaving abstract letter sounds into stories makes them interesting to young learners— activating the brain's positive emotional state and hooking the information into a strong memory template. In this way, SECRET STORIES® prompts learners' natural curiosity and triggers their "need to know" so as to actively engage them in the learning process.

Once students understand that SECRETS can help them to read and spell big, tricky "grown-up" words, they literally beg for more! Can you imagine a better situation than your students begging you to teach them more? SECRET STORIES® gives you the ability to meet their curiosity while arming them with the necessary tools to handle the patterns (and their exceptions) within text. Rather than giving up in frustration when they can't read or spell a word, students will begin asking for the SECRETS! This learner-driven model of SECRET STORIES® instruction will make teaching reading and writing the easiest and most satisfying content you will ever teach. Just remember to always take full advantage of the many teachable moments that SECRET STORIES® brings and make the most of each and every one!

It's much easier to think outside the box when you know what's in it, and learners who know the SECRETS own everything that's "in the box" when it comes to letters and the sounds they can make. SECRET STORIES® prepares learners for the incredibly complex task of accessing text by building upon their already existing social and emotional awareness and understanding. In this way, inexperienced readers quickly develop an easily accessible framework for decision-making about the most likely sounds of letters in unfamiliar text. For example, you'll find MOMMY E® and the BABYSITTER VOWELS® corralling SUPERHERO VOWELS®, and friendships between letters that change how they behave when they're together versus when they're hanging out on their own. Even the youngest child understands that when Mom (MOMMY E®) or a babysitter (BABYSITTER VOWEL®) is around, you do what you're told, unless you're far enough away that they can't reach you! But even then, the child knows that he can only get away with certain things. In letter speak, I like to say that "*a* is never going to go crazy and suddenly sound like a *k*, as there are only so many things that *a* can do, so let's read the word and see what sound

NEXT MOST LIKELY

Just as the apple won't fall far from the tree, a letter won't stray far from its sound. An *a* is never going to suddenly sound like a *k*, but it might be making its *next* most likely sound.

would make the most sense."

Aligning complex phonics skills to that which learners *already* understand enables young and struggling readers to quickly gain power over text, minimizing the learning curve by eliminating the need for repetitive, skill based practice. In this way, inexperienced readers are able to predict the "most" and "next most" likely sound behaviors for letters in text, just as they could easily predict the most likely behaviors of their friends and classmates.

A similar concept, known as Scenario-Based Training (SBT), is used by the military to help navigate decision-making of inexperienced soldiers through unfamiliar situations. Anchoring new information to already existing and familiar patterns is what allows inexperienced learners (like inexperienced soldiers) to navigate their way through unfamiliar text. It's learners' personal connection with the characters and their stories that allow them to discern between their most and next most likely sound behaviors— as they put themselves in the letters' shoes. This quickly emerging decision-making framework promotes both critical analysis and diagnostic thinking, so as to prepare young and inexperienced learners to effectively navigate unfamiliar text.

SECRET STORIES® brain based approach to phonics skill acquisition makes it one of the most highly effective reading instruction concepts available to educators, eliminating time-consuming sight word practice, memorization of phonics rules, and having to tell kids, *"It just is... It just does... You'll just have to remember..."* whenever they can't read or spell a word.

Simply put, SECRET STORIES® makes phonics make sense.

SECRET STORIES® Quick Start Guide

WHAT TO DO	WHY TO DO IT
Master individual letters and sounds by singing the Better Alphabet™ Song (with Eye-Glue and Muscle-Mouths!) twice a day, every day, for two weeks to two months. *page 36 (*Use access code on inside back cover to download the musical exercises.)*	Because learners encounter every letter, every sound, every day as they engage with text; and because muscle memory is a better and faster means of sound-skill retrieval than cognitive processing for early and/or struggling learners.
Hang ALL posters up before Day 1 so as to be ready to share what's needed to accomplish the reading, writing and spelling tasks at hand, as well as to increase learners' visual acuity for easier recognition of the patterns in text. *page 32*	Because SECRETS are introduced as they are needed and therefore must always be visually accessible; and because learners will be constantly scanning ALL of the posters when looking for the ones that they know— reinforcing visual recognition of all the SECRETS, even those that haven't yet been introduced.
Learners must always SEE what they SAY (or SING) in order to connect symbols to sounds, so remember to always reference the visual (i.e. individual letters on the alphabet train and/or the posters) *page 30*	Because what's used together becomes fused together in the brain, prompting formation of multi-layered memories for deeper learning connections and increased skill retention and retrieval.
Look for and take advantage of opportunities throughout the instructional day and across all content areas to both introduce and reinforce SECRETS—modeling their use to read or spell unknown words. *page 23 and 129*	Because the brain learns best on a "need to know" basis with learners driving their own instruction; and because presenting skills in context provides a meaningful and purposeful framework for use.
When unable to read or spell a word, ask learners if they see (or hear) a SECRET in it. . *page 26*	Because every SECRET learned is yet another tool in learners' ever expanding toolbox— and the more tools they bring to the table, the more value they will take away each day!

Using
The *Secret Stories*®

Introducing A Secret

There is no wrong way to tell a Secret, but there are good, better and best ways. It's important to keep in mind that *Secret Stories*® is not a program and therefore is not grade specific, nor does it hold back any skills from introduction. Rather, *Secret Stories*® are the tools learners need to crack the entire reading and writing code. Knowing the Secrets empowers even the youngest of learners (as well as those lagging behind at the upper grade levels) to read the books that they are genuinely interested in and to write the words that *they* desire in their stories.

Many teachers ask when they should start introducing Secrets and the answer is on the very first day. Do not wait for individual letter sound mastery to start sharing the Secrets! As said before, even preK and kindergarten learners are apt to come across *th* in text just as often— if not more than— *t* by itself. Thus, both are equally important. And this is the ideal perspective to have with regard to all other letters and phonics patterns as well, with each one being an equally important and necessary piece of a giant reading and writing puzzle…always keeping in mind that our goal as teachers is to provide learners with all of the pieces as early as possible. Just as a Morse Code operator can't do much with just a third or half of the code, neither can a reader or writer.

A Secret is most effectively introduced in context with existing daily curriculum and activities across the entire instructional day, not as a designated phonics lesson for the purpose of teaching isolated skills. Our brains don't learn like that! Instead, they learn best on a need-to-know basis. In other words, the brain learns best on its own agenda and for its own designated purpose.

There is no set time or instructional block during which the Secrets are best shared. Rather, they should be discovered,

PUSH AND PULL

The more Secrets learners know, the more they will want to know. This is the "Push and Pull" effect that emerges to become the driving force of Secret Stories® instruction. You'll start to hear, "There must be a Secret in that word!" immediately followed by the plea, "Please tell us what it is! *PLEEEEEASE!*"

ROLE-PLAY

Play the role of the learner, feigning shock upon discovery of yet another supposed contradiction in text (or on the calendar, a hallway sign, a milk carton, etc.). Simply say aloud (so as to effectively model this process), "There must be a SECRET in this word!" (in reference to the fact that a word cannot be sounded-out, or does not appear to be spelled correctly, based upon the SECRETS that learners know thus far.

told, and retold throughout the day, anywhere and anytime they are found hiding in text— writing lessons, reading activities, morning calendar, science books, math problems— even the cafeteria menu and daily strolls down the hall! There are endless opportunities for spotting, sharing, and applying SECRETS.

Think about your students. Let's say you've shared the SECRETS of the SUPERHERO VOWELS® with them and they realize now that only vowels can say their names. They should take issue with you the next time they see the word *art* on the activity calendar. You might hear their little voices say, "Hey, how come the *r* gets to say his name? He's not a superhero! You said that only the SUPERHERO VOWELS® could say their names!"

This would be the perfect moment to stop everything and share with the class that this word is so very tricky because it has a grown-up reading and writing secret hidden inside. Then, after a few seconds of appearing to silently debate whether or not they are actually big enough to hear such a grown-up SECRET, you can let them in on it. But, be sure to remind them not to tell any of their friends in other classes (*wink wink*) since they might not be grown-up enough to hear it!

There could be no more ideal time than this to add the *ar* SECRETS to students' existing repertoire of SECRETS. Their brains are ready to receive the information because they want to understand and piece together how this all works. And the more SECRETS learners know, the more apparent discrepancies they will notice, which creates even more teachable moments in which to share more SECRETS. A natural cycle emerges where the more they know, the more they will *want* to know.

If learners aren't yet picking up on these apparent contradictions in their daily experiences with text, you can encourage them to do so by modeling the role of an inquisitive learner (see page 26, "Steps For Reading/Decoding A Word"). Prompt learners to look for the holes in the logic of our language and to then call you on the carpet for the SECRETS as they notice them. Since our language is so seemingly random, this will occur almost constantly—which means students are critically analyzing and employing higher-level thinking skills as they interact with text throughout the entire instructional day. A teacher's dream! Engaging and motivating learners in this way only further prompts attentiveness to the skills being shared. Intrinsic motivation becomes the driving force as learners continue to engage their newly acquired skills for reading and writing purposes at hand. That's twice the brain-bang for your buck. Hooray!

Use what you need– when you need it!

A man stands at the counter of a hardware store, having just purchased the best tool kit in the store. He asks the clerk, "Excuse me, but when I get home, which of these tools should I use first?"

The store clerk looks at the man with a puzzled expression, replying, "Well sir, I guess that depends on what you need to fix. If your toilet's leaking, then you might want to use that wrench, but if it's a leaky faucet you've got, then I'd suggest you try the screwdriver. Now, if clogged-up pipes are the issue, then these pliers should do the trick. And if ever you just want to hang a picture, then use this hammer..."

The moral of this story is to consider SECRET STORIES® your phonics toolkit and to use what you need, when you need it, or— better yet— what your students need, the minute that they need it.

Reading And Writing With The SECRETS

You may be wondering why there's no order for introducing the SECRETS. Remember how I said earlier that our brains learn on a need-to-know basis? Well, you probably won't need to know what the letter *m* says (not for any reason I can think of, at least). But you may need to know how to write the word *mom* (on the birthday card you've made for her, or how to read the word *mom* on the book you want to read about her). The goal is to quickly fill learners' toolboxes, ensuring they have what they need, when they need it—so as to serve their own, personal reading and writing agendas. The next two pages model steps for both reading (decoding) a word and writing (encoding) a word.

STEPS FOR READING/DECODING A WORD

WRITING TRICKS

For activities to help learners capture the sounds they hear in words, see "Zookeeper" (pg. 27) and "Candy Quizzes" (pg. 28).

STEP 1: Say, "There must be a SECRET in the word if you can't sound it out."

STEP 2: Ask, "Do you see any SECRETS in it?" (In other words, "Do you see any letters in the word that are on any of the posters?")

STEP 3: Once the correct SECRET poster is spotted, ask learners to tell the story, encouraging dramatization of the sound and providing opportunities for the whole group to do the same.

STEP 4: Apply the secret sound to the word that learners are attempting to decode.

Zookeeper

If you were a zookeeper, and one day all of your animals escaped, you wouldn't just go out and try to catch the monkey and tiger and then call it a day?! I mean, what kind of zoo would you have with only a monkey and a tiger! Not a very good one, for sure! A good zookeeper must do his best to capture as *many* animals as he possibly can— as that is the only way to have the kind of zoo that others will want to visit! The same goes for writing a word— just like a good zookeeper must work to capture as many animals as possible, a good writer must work to capture as many *letters* as possible, so as to have a word that others will be able to read! Just jotting down a couple of letters and calling it a word is not what good writers do. Good writers listen for as many sounds and secrets as they can hear in a word, so as to capture as many letters in that word as possible! (And to really drive this point home, give students a "Candy Quiz.")

For a fun twist (and to reinforce the power of the SECRETS), encourage learners to sound out words both *with* and *without* the SECRETS. Let them do it correctly, with the SECRET sound, and then incorrectly, as they would have done before they knew its SECRET— making the sound for each letter in the word individually. This activity is very empowering for learners, as it reinforces the value of the SECRETS and the power that they are quickly gaining over text with each new SECRET learned.

STEPS FOR WRITING/ENCODING A WORD

Modeling use of the SECRETS for writing is similar to reading and is easily done in both whole and small group settings, either at the board or gathered around for a guided writing activity. I like to tell the kids they're going to be my brain, and that I can only write what they tell me, proceeding to write exactly what they say, letter by letter. While they do this, I think aloud about what to

TIPS AND TRICKS

Beginning writers don't always write down all of the letters they hear in words they are trying to write. The "Zookeeper" and "Candy Quiz" strategies are powerful tools for motivating learners to incorporate the SECRETS they know into words they want to write.

write next. In this way, I can play the role of a learner struggling to figure out which letter (or SECRET) comes next in a given word.

Take, for instance, the word *house*.

STEP 1: Say, "Well, I got the *h* sound for *h-h-house*, but there's no letter in the alphabet that says *owwww*! So I don't know what to do!" And then boohoo a little, depending on your grade level.

STEP 2: Look at the SECRET STORIES® posters and ask, "Do you see any letters that look like they are making the *owwww* sound based on the action in the picture?"

STEP 3: Say, "I see it! It's the *ow / ou*! Once the correct SECRET poster is spotted, ask learners to retell the story, encouraging dramatization of the sound and providing opportunities for the whole group to do the same.

STEP 4: After selecting the *ow* or *ou*, continue to model the role of a learner who does not know which of the two

Candy Quizzes

After playing "Zookeeper" your students are ready for a "Candy Quiz"! Just like a spelling test, but with no downside! Students can earn one candy (or reward token) for every letter (or SECRET) sound they can capture (write down) in a word. You can start off with just one word or two words, or use more if you like, as there is only positive reinforcement—no negative! So even struggling learners who may only be able to identify a handful of letter sounds are still rewarded for the ones they *do* know. Candy Quizzes are a fun and easy way to informally assess learners' level of skill ability and provide an ideal snapshot of letter/sound SECRET STORIES® skill awareness and application.

They also help to ensure that learners are able to *write* what they can *read*.

is correct. Next, let learners know that selecting either would be awesome, but that the grown-up way to spell it is with *ou*. (Notice I said grown-up way, not right way, so as not to discourage their attempts.)

FINE-TUNING SPELLING

It has been proven that experience with text is one of the best ways to fine-tune learner spelling, as the more Secrets learners know, the more they are able to read and write on their own, and the more text experience they accumulate. In this way, a sort of textual framework is established, providing an invaluable template upon which to build. This textual framework serves

by, mommy, July, candy, Monday

These words are common vocabulary in primary grade classrooms and will easily arise in daily conversation at various times throughout an instructional day. If the only sound shared so far for *y* is in words like *yo-yo* and *yellow*, then you now have a springboard into the ideal teachable moment for sharing the Secret about Sneaky Y® (pg. 68).

LESSON PLANS

Since Secrets aren't planned in advance, one easy way to document their instruction is to create a running record of those already shared in the form of a moveable index card. Simply clip to each weekly lesson plan, adding any new Secrets as they are shared, then re-clip to the next week's plans.

to naturally fine-tune beginning spelling rather than having to memorize words in their entirety. It is this basic level of skill mastery that enables even beginning readers to successfully read their own writing and further build upon it. Most importantly, learners possessing this ability to manipulate textual patterns in language will not be limited to writing only words that are familiar, (that is, controlled vocabulary, word-wall words, sight-words, etc.). They will instead be empowered to effectively express their ideas as they use the Secrets to write whatever words they choose to tell their stories.

No time wasted on repetitive and isolated skill practice means that learners have more time in which to engage in authentic text experiences that are personally meaningful and relevant to them, as they occur naturally and throughout the instructional day. There is simply no better way to reinforce newly acquired skills than to *use* them… with intention, for a genuinely meaningful purpose.

Body Intelligence

ACTION BASED LEARNING

3-PRONG APPROACH

SEE it!
SAY it!
DO it!

The SECRET STORIES® employ motor/muscle-memory and action-based cuing for acquisition of individual letter sounds, as well as for bypassing common early learner-issues of developmental readiness, processing and/or language delays. As concrete learners, young children learn best by touching and doing. Using purpose-driven movements within a contextualized story compels the learner to take on a more active and participatory role, rather than be relegated to the traditional, more passive one. Each and every one of the SECRET STORIES® presented supports a variety of opportunities for kinesthetic movement (mobility), ranging from a naturally occurring simple gesture when sharing a SECRET, or a deliberate cueing motion that directs the learner to a specific sound (referred to as an Action Cue, and you'll see one for every SECRET contained in this book). Encouraging meaningful mobility in this purpose driven and contextualized way provides yet another learning channel through which these new skills may be directly woven into the learner.

James Asher, father of Total Physical Response (TPR), says that,

"For many learners, the body's intelligence exceeds cognitive ability." This is often the case with early learners, due to challenges associated with developmental readiness, as well as with non-native English speaking students. Studies prove that the body remembers as well as the mind, and even better for some learners. Thus, for many struggling learners, the inherent motor/muscle-memory is often a more reliable means for skill acquisition than is actual cognitive processing capability.

The components of the SECRET STORIES® that really drive home action-based learning are the posters and the musical brain teasers, which are demonstrated on the music download. The graphic actions on the posters are designed to prompt their respective sounds. They employ muscle-memory and/or action-based cues designed to land learners in the sounds rather than commit them to memory. The Better Alphabet™ Song (see inside back cover for the download code) trains the lips, tongue, and teeth to build up their muscle-memory, as well as to increase sound-skill automaticity. When singing "Mary Had a Little Lamb" enough times, you don't have to worry about them saying "Mary had a little duck" because your mouth literally won't let the wrong word come out. These are examples of body intelligence at its best!

ACTIVE LEARNING

"99% of what we learn in life, we learn through mobile experience, and not in front of a classroom chalkboard."

–James Asher

The Posters

You'll see how easy it is to weave the SECRETS through all of the different subject areas across the instructional day as you become more familiar with them. They fit perfectly within what's already going on in your classroom, making it easy to follow the number one cardinal rule— always share in the context of what you're already teaching and/or the students need to know.

Making sure the visuals are all easily accessible and ready to share from the very beginning gives students immediate access to skills as they come up, which often happens unexpectedly, throughout the course of daily instruction. Even in kindergarten, teachers should have all the posters hung and ready so they're prepared whenever an opportunity presents itself to share a SECRET. Additionally, by visually immersing learners in these common phonemic patterns, their visual acuity is greatly enhanced, allowing them to more easily spot them in text, even before they are formally introduced. Providing these valuable opportunities for pre-exposure to skills, even before formal instruction has occurred, is yet another crucial element of brain-based teaching of tremendous value to *all* learners.

WHERE SHOULD I HANG THEM?

The posters are best placed in a location that allows learners the easiest visual access to them at all times of the day. Keep in mind that students will be referencing them constantly throughout the day during whole group, small group, and guided activities and instruction.

There is no specific order with regard to their placement, with

ALL POSTERS UP

The only exception is preschool, where teachers can begin with the foundational ones (SUPERHERO VOWELS®, SNEAKY Y®, and MOMMY E®) and hang additional SECRETS as they are discovered and introduced.

While the larger sized posters are ideal for display in the primary grade classrooms, the smaller sized, *Dual-Use Placards* are a great option for hands-on manipulative use in circle time, guided reading, Centers, etc.

the exception of the Superhero Vowels®, Sneaky Y®, and *qu* posters, which should be hung just above those same letters on your already existing classroom alphabet to reinforce their unique capabilities and alternate sound options.

All other posters should be hung together, or in close proximity of one another, so as to minimize learner effort in referencing them. If desired, they may be grouped according to their most likely position within a word— beginning, middle, or end. For example, you might choose to cluster *th, sh, wh, ch,* etc… in one general area, and *ing, ed, ion, tion/sion,* etc… in another. This will not work for all the Secrets, but it will provide some basis for general placement. As said before, there is no right way, aside from just making sure that all are displayed and easily accessible.

INCREASING THE BUZZ

You can really increase the buzz among students by displaying extra sets of *Secret Stories®* posters in common areas throughout the school, or anywhere students line-up and wait, like the cafeteria line, hallways, media center, front office, etc. This prompts learner discussion and provides valuable opportunities for continued visual exposure to these critical phonemic patterns. It's also an easy way to let parents in on what the Secrets actually are and how they work, as they can't help but notice them, and then ask the kids. The Secrets should be viewed by the learners as a sort of reading treat, something they must earn the right to hear as a result of super thinking, effort, behavior, etc…

Of course, you as their teacher become the keeper of all that is secret. You can decide whether or not to tell the learners the Secret they are obviously now dying to know.

IT'S A SECRET!

As there's no official order for telling the Secrets, different classrooms will learn them at different times– intensifying learner secretiveness and further prompting learner dialogue and excitement.

Blending Brain Teasers

DECODING DITTIES

Don't view these musical brain teasers as static songs to be sung repetitively without variation and on autopilot. Instead, see them as creative, constantly changing ditties, offering both interactive and manipulative decoding and encoding practice that motivates learners to think fast and stay on their toes– and thereby remain in their optimal learning mode. Access using the download code on the back cover and see page 159 for more.

Use the download code on the inside back cover of your book to access the Better Alphabet™ and Brain Teaser Blending Songs. These musical exercises are designed to strengthen the critical connection between speech and print in the brain by rapidly moving from "sound to symbol" and "symbol to sound." Using music to mimic the processes of both decoding and encoding helps to build speed and automaticity for reading and writing.

Additionally, research shows that by integrating music into instruction, learners are able to meet difficult challenges with minimal stress. They can remain comfortable, while at the same time, be highly challenged. This combination of "high challenge" and "low stress" prompts what research refers to as the "flow state," or optimal learning mode—the absolute perfect combination for learning to best occur. (See next page for more on this.)

Rather than relying on repetitious skill practice through static songs, all but the very first track in the music download is intended to be used as a guided listening tool to help you create your own musical combinations for the many letters, sounds, and SECRETS. While it is true that repetition can build muscle-memory, it's important to understand that building automaticity requires more than just mere replication of the same song over and over again. Think of the child who has learned the months of the year using a little ditty that starts with January and ends at December. When asked what comes after August, you'll likely hear him start at January and sing straight through at least

The Optimal Learning Experience

In order to truly own information, a learner must be able to both easily and effectively manipulate it. The auditory manipulations on the *Secret Stories*® music download serve this function well. They provide support for instruction by allowing the learner to meet difficult challenges with minimal stress— even when the challenge presented exceeds the learner's ability level. Research shows that the integration of music with skill manipulation (not musical regurgitation) minimizes learner stress. It provides opportunities for best matching learner ability with respective skill level for the most effective practice. In this way, learners are able to manipulate skills to their highest level of ability with minimal stress, while remaining in what is referred to as optimal learning mode, or "flow state," which occurs directly between the states of boredom and anxiety.

Think of it as a "relaxed-peaked" state, or a "peaked-relaxation." I refer to learners in this state as wearing their "catch-a-ball" faces, as this is the best way to describe their facial expression when engaged in musical exercises—a sort of "hyper-focused" state of alert! While in this state, learner-attention is laser focused, action and awareness merge, and all aspects of performance are heightened. Thinking becomes fluid and flexible, and anxiety disappears— even for lower-level learners who might otherwise struggle. For further reading on optimal learning and the flow state, see "Evidence Base" (pg. 155), *Research on Memory and Learning*, by Mihaly Csikszentmihalyi.

To get familiar with how it works, listen to the musical blending brain teaser exercises on the download prior to sharing them with your students. While you listen, read through the next few pages to see how to plug the skills into the lyrics for each musical brain teaser, as well as how to easily increase the difficulty level by switching them up, so as to move each exercise from basic letter/sound mastery, to more complex blending of the sound patterns within the *SECRET*.

September (often having to do so multiple times) in order to correctly answer the question. So while skill repetition in the form of a static song does help learners build muscle-memory, it is of less value when considering one has to go all the way back to the beginning in order to retrieve the information needed.

Like every other part of the *SECRET STORIES®* you can tailor these musical brain teasers to suit your needs as you continue to share more and more *SECRETS* with your students. I used readily familiar melodies that may be sung easily, without having to use the music for accompaniment, as that is not its purpose. Instead, these later tracks serve as templates for varied letter/sound/pattern skill retrieval, manipulation, and practice— from simple to more difficult, building learners' sound-skill automaticity as they rapidly move from sound to symbol (for reading) and symbol to sound (for writing), manipulating the *SECRET STORIES®* randomly. Used in this way, these musical brain teasers may be easily integrated into your existing instructional framework, providing yet another connection for learners. Ultimately, you will transfer these newly acquired phonics skills into reading and writing tools the students can own forever.

In addition to the examples for each musical brain teaser, I've included notes about how to use each track. The tracks incorporate varied and progressive skill levels for each exercise, from basic letter/ sound mastery to blending the *SECRET STORIES®* sounds.

TRACK 1: ("THE 'BETTER' ALPHABET™ SONG")

For anyone working with learners who don't yet know all of the individual letters and sounds, this song should be your first priority. Sing this first track of the download (access code on inside back cover) with your class every day, morning and afternoon, for at least two weeks (continuing up to the two-month mark if needed). Unlike all other tracks, this one actually *is* sung in the form of static song (but without the downside, which I will explain) and as such, should be sung with repetition, and in the same way every time. Its purpose is not to manipulate skills, but rather to train the lips, tongue, and teeth to find them. Doing so allows us to bypass areas of weakness, such as developmental or cognitive readiness in early learners, and tap into areas of strength (body intelligence). This track builds muscle memory, as the lips, tongue, and teeth follow a familiar pathway from letter to sound. The result is often of great surprise to learners, as even when they doubt they know how a letter sounds, their mouths' muscles easily take them to it.

The tune for this first track repeats itself for every single letter, so there is no need to go back to *a* to remember how *x* sounds. Thus, learners can start singing right on the letter they need (when unsure of a letter's sound/sounds) and their lips, tongue, and teeth will guide the way.

Before leading your class in singing this first track, you need to remind them of two very important things. First, they must always *see what they sing* (see "Eye-Glue" pg 39). In other words, learners must look at a letter when singing its sound. Second, they must fully engage their mouth muscles by over-enunciating the sounds when singing them (see "Muscle-Mouth" pg 39).

You will also notice a shadow schwa ("uh") sound following some of the consonants on this track. The reason for this is explained on "The 'Better' Alphabet™ Song" lyrics page in the text box (see the "Shadow Schwa" on pg 160).

INDIVIDUAL LETTER SOUNDS

"The 'Better' Alphabet™ Song" (Track 1) is the only musical exercise sung as an actual song. Its purpose is to activate learners' muscle-memory as the primary means of individual letter and sound skill retrieval.

MUSCLE MEMORY

Studies prove that the body remembers as well as the mind, and even better for some learners! This is especially true for very young and/or struggling learners for whom muscle memory is often the more reliable means for skill acquisition than cognitive processing.

TRACKS 2–5: THE LETTER RUNS

Similar to the first track, these four tracks focus on rapid retrieval of the individual letter sounds only (as opposed to singing the letters names with the sounds). They raise the bar to a higher level of letter and sound skill retrieval, and are designed to mimic the decoding process. Learners will see the letters and make their sound, all while singing at varying speeds.

TRACKS 6–22: SKILL ACQUISITION

The rest of the download provides for rapid manipulation and retrieval of all of the letter sounds and *SECRET STORIES*® patterns.

Blend Bracelets & *SECRET STORIES*® Necklaces

For easy, portable visual reference when singing the musical brain teasers outside the classroom (or in small group, circle time, etc.) make some assessment jewelry! Write all of the individual letters (capitals on one side, lower case letters on the other) on small index cards, punch a hole in the upper right corner, and then string together with thin strips of fabric or ribbon.

You can create an entire "jewelry collection" that can be worn anywhere— to lunch, in the hallway, on a field trip, to parent pick up, etc. As the children progress through the various skill levels, more jewelry may be created to include: blend bracelets, *SECRET STORIES*® necklaces, and even outlaw accessories.

Hang your assessment jewelry in a convenient location near the door in your classroom so as to grab and go!

Use your jewelry often and spontaneously, anytime and every time possible, especially during the downtimes of your day when the students are waiting. These Jewelry Assessment Tools provide a convenient and consistent means to ensure students always see what they sing, supporting the ability and likelihood of truly addressing *"every letter, every sound, everyday!"*

LEARNERS MUST SEE WHAT THEY SING

Always make visual reference to the individual letters while singing each of the sounds. Learners must always see what they sing. Be sure to point to the letters (or SECRETS) on the wall whenever singing their sounds. Both the capital and the lowercase forms of each letter should be depicted on whatever alphabet visual you use so you can reference both at the same time when singing a letter's sound/sounds. It's important to also scrutinize the pictures that are supposed to prompt each of the sounds to ensure that they actually show its most likely one. (For example, the letter *x* should not be depicted with a picture of a xylophone, as it's most likely to say *-ks*, as in *box, ox,* or *fox*…not *zzzzz!*)

ACTIVATING MUSCLE-MEMORY

When relying on muscle-memory to find and feel the sounds of the letters, it's important to remind learners to really work their lips, tongue, and teeth. You want them to over-exaggerate the sounds so as to fully engage their muscle-memory. The best way to make this happen is to model over-articulating the sounds as you sing along with them. (Just keep in mind that by doing so, learners will be more inclined to look at you than the letters that they are singing as you will be fascinating to watch!) Tell learners that by building up super strong lip, tongue, and teeth muscles, they won't have to *learn* the letters and sounds, as their muscles will do the work for them. And to up the ante, tell them that you will be giving a "Muscle-Mouth Award."

Likewise, to ensure learners always look at the letters when singing their sounds, you can award a student (or students) with the "Eye-Glue Award" for doing the best job of never taking their eyes off

EYE-GLUE & MUSCLE-MOUTHS

Encourage learners to see what they sing and build muscle memory for easy letter sound retrieval with friendly competitions for the "Eye-Glue" and "Muscle-Mouth" Awards!

them as they are singing. I found that the best way to do this on a daily basis was to make it a contest between the boys and the girls, with the winning group earning coveted privileges, like being the first to line up, or first to select their Centers, etc. This rivalry was key to maintaining learners' overall focus and attention throughout the entire song, and ensure they not only know the sounds for each letter but also what each looks like.

As with the "Eye-Glue Award," the "Muscle-Mouth Award" serves a similar purpose by encouraging learners to fully engage their mouth muscles when singing the sounds. The goal is to encourage activation of learners' muscle-memory for easy sound retrieval. This, too, can be done as an individual award or as an ongoing contest between the boys and the girls, seeing who can work their lips, tongue, and teeth the hardest.

SUMMER REVIEW

Tell parents to save all SECRET Sheets that students bring home for use as a cumulative SECRET Summer Review Packet.

SECRET Skill Sheets

The reproducible SECRET Sheets (located in the back of this book) are best utilized during small or guided group times, with students of like-level abilities working through them together, taking turns sounding out the words. As a child is taking his turn, attacking a particular word's letter/pattern aloud, all of the others should be following along by pointing to the letters on their own sheets. The opportunity to both point to and see the letters, without the responsibility of having to actually make the sound, provides an invaluable practice opportunity for the other students around the table. All students must actively follow along with their fingers (or with special "magic" pointers— slim colored pencils, highlighters, etc…) when not reading aloud. Those who don't should not be allowed to remain with their group and must wait until next time to try for mastery of their SECRET Sheet. It

A Word About Guided Reading And Authentic Assessments

Teaching in context supports the premise that good literature should be put into the hands of children as early as possible. A great way to make sure this happens with your students is to establish guided reading groups (four to six students you can meet with at least once per day). Students can participate in shared reading, writing, and discussion of appropriate leveled trade books, in addition to your existing reading text series.

Guided reading groups also offer valuable opportunities to assess more accurately and with greater specificity individual student needs. You can then use those findings to further drive your instruction accordingly. It is desirable to have students with similar skill levels in each guided reading group, as text level and challenge must be dictated by the individual skill levels of the students within each group. For some group activities, however, such as guided literature discussion, a student group with varied levels of reading and skill proficiency may offer greater support in overall text recognition, as well as fostering a creative group dynamic in shared story discussion. These groups provide further opportunities for the engagement of students in meaningful and purposeful language experiences that may be used to assess skill mastery in a specific area, commonly referred to as authentic assessments (that is, literature based reading/writing activities, reading/writing with a "real world" purpose, such as comprehension assessment of a newspaper article or preparing a grocery list for spelling assessment).

It is not necessary for phonemic skill mastery to be achieved prior to beginning such shared group experiences, or even prior to guided group reading of appropriately leveled text and trade books. Although it is true that prior to the learner achieving some level of phonemic skill awareness, he will be more likely to memorize text patterns, using primarily only picture clues to establish meaning. A beginning reader might also make use of context clues and syntax (that is, what makes sense and starts with that letter). These are good questions that good readers should be asking themselves when working with unfamiliar text. The ability of a reader to self-monitor implies that the learner is aware of the primary purpose of reading for meaning.

is extremely important to impress upon your students that this is a grown-up reading group, focused on grown-up, "secret" reading, and therefore only grown-up, super-student behavior is acceptable.

At the early grade levels, guided groups should remain flexible, due to the constantly changing levels of student readiness and ability levels. Allow early learners to progress at their own pace through each successive SECRET Sheet before moving on to the next. Once mastered, students may take their SECRET Sheet home to share with parents, along with the blank sheet that allows further opportunities to look for and apply the SECRETS they've mastered.

Keep in mind that some learners will work in group on mastery of a given SECRET Sheet several times before proficiency is determined and the sheet is sent home; while others may move through a given SECRET Sheet on the first attempt and move immediately to the next. It is not unusual for stronger readers to initially progress independently through multiple sheets/skills at a time, before reaching one that is actually targeting their instructional/challenge level. This may result in some students, temporarily, being in a group by themselves, should they be the only one working on mastery of a given SECRET Sheet. Likewise, as students move about at varying paces from one group to another, there may be times where too many students are stuck on the same sheet, requiring you to break them into more manageable groups of six or seven.

It's also important to keep in mind that for some more advanced readers, their progression through the various SECRET Sheets may actually *surpass* your SECRET STORIES® whole group instruction. In this case, it is perfectly appropriate, and encouraged, to introduce the SECRET directly to those working on that particular skill sheet, as assessment of learner need should always be the driving force behind your instruction.

SECRET STARS

Students will beg to be called to your guided reading table for a chance to earn a SECRET Star! Students can earn a coveted SECRET Star for each SECRET Sheet mastered. They can then collect and trade these SECRET Stars for privileges or rewards each nine weeks. Students won't want to miss their chance to progress to the next level, and they'll be vying to get called up to try for a SECRET Star!

Using SECRET Skill Sheets

Motivate learners with SECRET Stars earned for each SECRET Sheet mastered! These coveted stars (which can be traded in for prizes or classroom privileges) provide the perfect incentive for learners to voluntarily give up bits of free time, Center activities, etc. to come up to your table (or with a parent volunteer) and try for mastery of a SECRET Sheet. Seldom do students ever decline the opportunity to try for another SECRET Star! You will soon have students coming up to you throughout the day, begging for their SECRET group to be called later that afternoon. This also provides a wonderful behavior incentive since you can only call so many groups up each day.

Keep in mind that only some in each group are ready to earn stars, while others may need a bit more practice to attain star-level proficiency. All members of a group will almost never learn a SECRET Star at the same time, and only those who do will move on to the next sheet/level.

Those who do may take home their SECRET Sheet, put their name on the next one to be mastered, and place it in the next-leveled groups' file so you can call them up with that new group the next time. Those needing a few more practice rounds for mastery can mark the date practiced (to keep track of the total number of times) and then place theirs back into the folder with those still working toward mastery of the same SECRET Sheet.

Be sure to let parents know that they should be on the look out for these coveted SECRET Sheets/Stars, and that kids deserve lots of kudos for each one earned! These SECRET Sheets provide a jumping point from which students may share the SECRETS they know with their parents!

Teachers And Parents

Supplemental materials, such as SECRET STORIES® *Porta-Pics* and *Parent-Home Version*, are available for more comprehensive parent involvement and easy home sharing. However, even without these supplemental resources there are other easy ways to share the SECRETS with parents. I recommend giving your students a special challenge for sharing what they've learned at school once they're home. Whatever weekly communication tool you use with the parents, let them know their child has a special, grown-up reading and writing SECRET to share with them. You can also use the SECRET Sheets' word lists at the back of this book (pg. 179) to track learning in the classroom, as well as to send home and give students the chance to show off their reading skills to their parents.

PARENT-HOME VERSION & PORTA-PICS

Those who want to use the SECRET STORIES® for at-home learning, either along with their child's classroom teacher or as homeschooling parents, will find that the same classroom concepts apply. Both the SECRET STORIES® *Parent-Home Version* and the *Porta-Pics* provide easy reference to the skills reinforced by the SECRET STORIES® when reading and writing at home.

While the SECRET STORIES® will be used by learners for many purposes (and by multi-age siblings) at home, they are most helpful for use in completing homework assignments where learners must read, write, or spell, including word problems in math or written answers in science. Parents should ask their child to point out the SECRETS they know, whenever and wherever they're spotted in text, and then to refer to the SECRET STORIES® pictures (found in the back of this book) to identify their sounds.

HOMEWORK

Dear Parents,

This week we ran across the word *August* on our word calendar. Ask your child to tell you the grown-up reading and writing SECRET that's in the word *August,* and see how many other words they can spot over this weekend that also have this special SECRET.

A great time to look for new SECRETS to share is when reading a book to or with your child, particularly when reading a nighttime story. Your child can read to you, or even just watch over your shoulder as you read. Seeing the SECRETS in context reinforces the ones they've already learned and gives them a great opportunity to spot new ones. Reading aloud with your child (regardless of age) offers a myriad of opportunities for sharing SECRETS. It's an ideal way, especially for beginning learners, to discover and learn about the *SECRET STORIES*®.

In no time, you and your child will be spotting SECRETS everywhere. Encourage their attempts to sound out and spell unfamiliar words, and when asked, "What's that word?" or "How do I spell it?" don't give them the answer. Instead, give them the SECRET.

It's also important to model how to use the SECRETS for your child. When modeling, you are playing the role of the learner, attempting to sound out or spell unfamiliar words. Role-playing in this way will further familiarize your child with the process of using the *SECRET STORIES*® for both reading and writing.

Remember, when you share the SECRETS at home, you are letting learners in on a grown-up reading and writing secret. This is the key to motivating their interest. In addition, always ensure that learners have easy visual access to the *SECRET STORIES*® pictures, located in the back of this book as cut-apart cards. Your child must be able to easily reference them whenever and wherever they will be reading or writing.

HOME VERSION VS. PORTA-PICS

The main difference between these two resources for home use is that the *Parent-Home Version* includes the stories and music download, thus allowing for at-home remediation and/or acceleration, as per learner-need; whereas the *Porta-Pics* simply provide a portable reference for reading and writing.

CUT-APART CARDS

For directions on how to turn the Cut-Apart Cards in the back of this book into a tri-fold, turn to page 217.

SECRET STORIES®
– CLASSIFIED –

Key to Using the SECRET STORIES®

This section contains the heart of SECRET STORIES®. The layout is simple and clean, allowing you to quickly access the story for the SECRET, action cue, and sound for each letter or pattern, as well as any other considerations or teaching tips.

This story information contained in the red section of the book corresponds with the graphic visuals (posters, cut-apart cards, or *Porta-Pics*) which are also on red, and that students will be referencing when using these skills.

To protect the intellectual property of this material, please do not make copies of these pages, retype the stories, or share the images. *Porta-Pics* are available if you would like to send home the visuals with students so that parents have the visual reference for each SECRET.

These are the "secrets" that explain why the letters make the different sounds that they do, and in a way that kids can connect with and remember!

SECRET

NAVIGATING THIS SECTION:

Here's the key to the symbols and elements used throughout these red pages.

When you tie the story to an action or emotion, you are activating multiple pathways, or modalities for learning. This increases learner automaticity of sound-skill retrieval. You'll find a short action or sequence of actions to go along with each story.

MEMO NOTE - These are special things to remember or think about regarding each SECRET. Each note has its own category, represented by one of the three icons shown to the right.

Just so you know!

Don't forget to tell the kids...

Mouth Shape / Sound Production

CLASSIFIED

© 2020 Marenem

SUPERHERO VOWELS®.

There are five letters in the alphabet that are actually superheroes! They have a power that no other letters have—they can SAY THEIR NAMES!

They are the SUPERHERO VOWELS®.

A, E, I, O and U!

But like all superheroes, they have secret identities (a.k.a. "short and lazy" disguises) to avoid being recognized!

© 2020 MARENEM

Raise up your arms and show off your "big muscles" when making the sounds of the SUPERHERO VOWELS®!

To avoid drawing attention to their superhero status, each vowel has its own "short and lazy" disguise. When they aren't using their superpowers to say their names, they will make their short and lazy sounds instead, so they're not recognized!

MOMMY E® and BABYSITTER VOWELS® (pgs 64-66) help kids know whether vowels will be long or short in words. But sometimes, even superheroes don't do what they should! So, if you ever see a vowel that's NOT making its correct sound, it might be because it's still thinking..."Should I be long?...Should I be short?...I just don't know....uhhhhh?" And "UHHH" is the sound that comes out! (was, of, come, was, want, about, want)
(See more on page 62.)

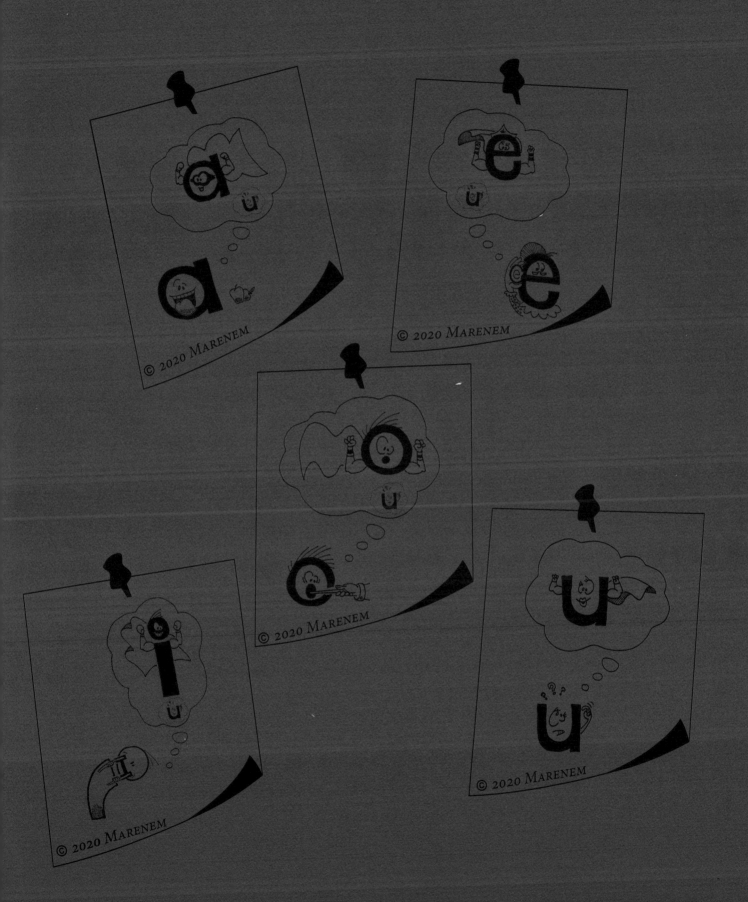

SUPERHERO a...

When a is in his short and lazy disguise, he will just sit around all day, munching on his favorite fruit...

Apples, of course! He knows that an apple a day keeps the doctor away, and he doesn't want to end up like his friend, SUPERHERO o! (pg 60)

"AA-AA-Apple!" And that's the sound he makes!

at, sat, cat

ACTION!!

To hook into a's short and lazy sound, hold an imaginary apple to your mouth, as if you are about to take a big bite! It's the moment just BEFORE the actual bite that your mouth is in the perfect short-a position. Your tongue is pulled back and your top jaw is lifted, so as to be ready to bite down into the apple. From this position, your mouth is set to make the perfect short-a, apple-bite "AAAA" sound. (Hint: For some kids, it helps to use a real apple! Just remember to have them freeze the moment BEFORE the actual bite!)

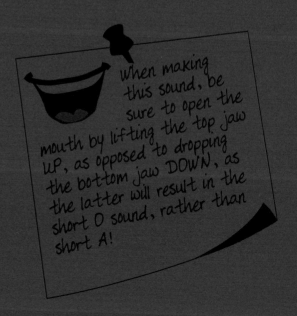

When making this sound, be sure to open the mouth by lifting the top jaw UP, as opposed to dropping the bottom jaw DOWN, as the latter will result in the short O sound, rather than short A!

© 2020 MARENEM

...and his short and lazy disguise

SUPERHERO e...

When e is in her short and lazy disguise, she pretends she's a little old lady who can't hear.

She will plop an old-lady bun on her head, put on some big glasses, and constantly interrupt everyone's conversation—

"EHHHH? Whad'ya say? EHHHH?" And that's the sound she makes!

ten, red, then

To hook into e's short and lazy sound, simply pretend to be a little old lady who can't hear! Cup your ear with your hand and then holler out (in your best old lady voice!) "EHHHH? Whad'ya say? EHHHH?"

When cupping your ear and pretending you can't hear (like short and lazy E) your ear will resemble the shape of lowercase "e"!

© 2020 MARENEM

...and her short and lazy disguise

SUPERHERO i...

When i is in his short and lazy disguise, he can be found exercising, as his superhero suit is getting a bit too tight!

His all-time favorite exercise is bending sideways at the waist while saying,

"IHH-IHH-IHH!" (with his mouth in the shape of a capital I). And that's the sound he makes!

it, sit, kids

© 2020 MARENEM

ACTION!!

To hook into Superhero i's short and lazy sound, put pointer fingers on the corners of your mouth and bend sideways at the waist while saying "IHH-IHH-IHH" and then bending to the other side and repeating several times. (When bent sideways, your mouth will look like a capital I!)

It's important to make sure that lips remain straight as a stick, as if opened up even a little, the sound will shift from "IHHH" to "EHHH" (short E). So be sure to keep those lips as "straight as a stick!"

Tell kids "If you put a finger here, and a finger here, and you turn sideways, your mouth looks like a capital I!" (See graphic.)

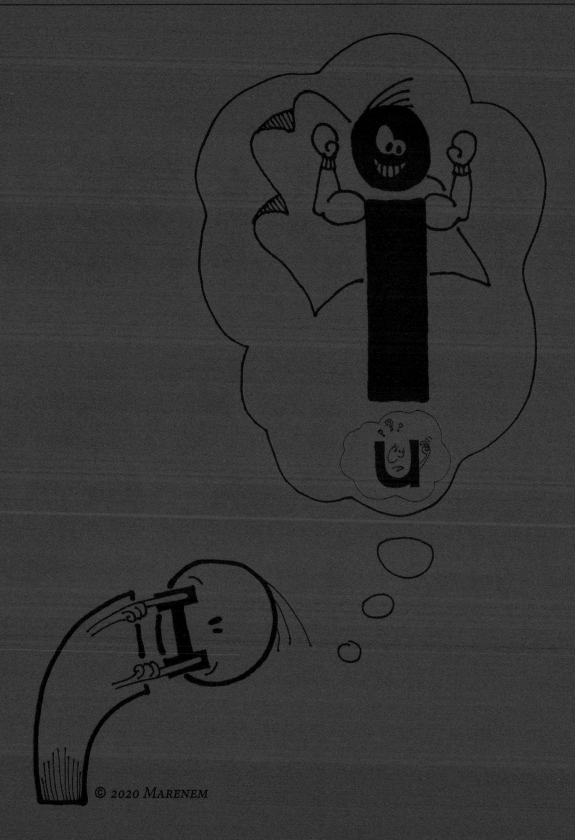

© 2020 MARENEM

...and his short and lazy disguise

SUPERHERO o...

When o is in his short and lazy disguise, he's always at the doctor's, as  he's always worried he's getting sick. He won't touch anything because he's afraid of germs! He's especially worried about the stick the doctor uses to check his throat. (He's not sure he always remember to throw it away between patients!) To be safe, he never lets his lips, tongue or teeth touch the yucky stick- "AHHHHHH!" And that's the sound he makes!

on, not, mop

© 2020 MARENEM

To hook into o's short and lazy sound, pretend your finger is the "yucky stick" (tongue depressor). Put it in your mouth and say "AHHHHHHH!" (Just be sure to keep it far away from your lips, tongue, and teeth so you don't touch the "yucky stick!" If you do it right, your mouth looks like an o!)

Always remember (and be sure to tell the kids!) to keep far away from the yucky stick, as if the jaw relaxes even a little, the "AHH" sound will collapse into the "UHH" (short U) sound instead!

Tell kids "That stick could have been in the mouth of the guy who just threw up all over the floor!" (While unpleasant, this ensures that kids will make the perfect short O sound every time!)

© 2020 MARENEM

...and his short and lazy disguise

SUPERHERO u...

When u is in her short and lazy disguise, she pretends to be a student who never listens to the teacher, and so she never knows what's going on.

SECRET

Whenever the teacher asks her a question, she scratches her head, looks confused, and responds,

"UHHHHHHHHH?" And that's the sound she makes!

up, run, cut

© 2020 MARENEM

ACTION!!

To hook into Superhero u's short and lazy sound, simply pretend that you don't know the answer to a question. Just scratch your head, look confused, and say, "UHHHHH?"

Superhero u actually pays excellent attention in class, just like superheroes do! She just pretends not to be listening so that no one suspects that she's actually a superhero!

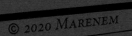

"Thinking Vowels / Head-Bop Trick"
When vowels can't decide whether to be long or short, they have to think about it...and while they're thinking, they say, "UHHHHHH?" (like short u). Sometimes, they bop themselves on the side of the head to help them think! You can use this "head-bop" gesture to remind kids to use this "Thinking Vowel" strategy to help them decode read tricky words, like: what, want, was, of, love, some, come, does, around, about among, something, and even pencil! (See page 52 for more.)

© 2020 MARENEM

...and her short and lazy disguise

Mommy E®

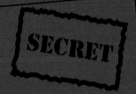

When Mommy E® sits at the end of a word, or is one letter away from another vowel, she will tell that vowel, "You say your name!" Then she covers her mouth and won't talk.

But, if Mommy E® is NOT at the end of a word, or is MORE than one letter away from another vowel, that vowel gets to be short and lazy...just like you'd be if your mommy weren't right there, close enough to make sure that you do what you should!

tape/tap, hope/hop, cute/cut
super/supper biter/bitter

© 2020 MARENEM

ACTION!!

When telling the Mommy E® story, shake your finger at the the vowel that's one letter away while saying, "You say your name!" and then slap your hand over your mouth to show that Mommy E® won't talk anymore!

(And don't forget to use the short and lazy actions for the short vowel sounds when Mommy E® is NOT at the end, or is too far away to make them say their names!)

In words like "have" or "river," Mommy E® is NOT doing her job and making the vowel say its name, but these are easy fixes! Simply tell the kids, "Sometimes Mommy's there, but she's too tired to care!" which means that the vowel can stay SHORT and LAZY! Encouraging learners to try the "next" most likely sound option helps them develop the flexible thinking that's needed when working with text. These easy-to-fix words are referred to to as "acceptable exceptions!" (See page 137.)

The SECRET STORIES® explain letter sounds based on their "most likely" and "next-most likely" behaviors. In this way, kids can easily identify and work through all likely sound options for letters in text.

a e
i
o
u

© 2020 MARENEM

BABYSiTTER VOWELS®

Sometimes MOMMY E® just has to get out of the house! And when she does, she'll put one of the vowels in charge and make them babysit.

So, if you ever see ANY vowel that's one letter away from another vowel, that's the babysitter! And it will do exactly what Mommy would if she were there, which is to tell the vowel,

"You say your name!"

making, biking, motor

ACTION!!

Do what Mommy would do if she were there. Shake your finger at the vowel that's one letter away while telling it, "You say your name!"

SNEAKY Y® can also babysit, but he doesn't like to, so he won't do it very often. But when he does, he tells any vowel that's one letter away to say its name!

(baby, lady, lazy)

© 2020 Marenem

SNEAKY Y®

Y got sick and tired of saying "YUH" all the time, so he snuck into the closets SUPERHERO e and SUPERHERO i and took one of each of their super capes! So now, whenever he's at the END of a word (and thinks no one can see him!) he will always be sneaky and wear either his e or i cape—so he can say THEIR name, instead!

mommy, daddy, by, my

But when he's at the BEGINNING of a word, he's a good little line leader, and does exactly what he should, which is say "Yuh!"

yellow, yes, you

© 2020 MARENEM

Stand up tall and straight (like a good little line leader!) and say, "YY-YY-YY" to show how SNEAKY Y® is on his best behavior and making the sound that he should when at the beginning of a word.

If you hear an E or an I sound at the end of a word that you're trying to spell, it's probably SNEAKY Y®!

(mommy, daddy, July, by)

© 2020 MARENEM

i Tries e On For Size

SECRET

While out for a walk one day, SUPERHERO i stumbled upon SUPERHERO e's cape, and he just couldn't resist trying it on for size!

He liked it so much, he decided to keep it, which is why i can sometimes be found making e's sound. If you look carefully, you just might catch him!

medium, serious, immediate

© 2020 MARENEM

ACTION!!

Hold up an imaginary cape and pretend to look at it as if you're just dying to try it on!

Maybe the reason that I wanted to try E's cape on was that his was getting too tight from all the cookies that E's been feeding him! (See page 120.) It's a good thing that I likes to exercise! (See page 58.)

This story also helps to explain the SECRET sound for IE, and why E is not very happy with I! (See page 120.)

© 2020 MARENEM

Two Vowels Go A-Walkin'

When these vowels® go a-walkin', the first one does the talkin' and it always says its name! (The second one covers its mouth and stays quiet.)

SECRET

ee, ea, ai, oa, ui, ue

feet, beat, bait,

boat, suit, blue

But sometimes, when ea walk together, e's too tired to say her name, so she makes her short & lazy sound instead!

head, ready, bread

© 2020 MARENEM

ACTION!!

Tell this story in a rhythmic way, almost chant-like. Pair kids up to walk as if they are the vowels, letting the first one say his name while the second covers her mouth.

This SECRET applies only to the vowel pairs shown, as vowel pairs in other Secrets make different sounds.

Remember to always try the most likely sound first, before moving on to the "next-most likely" ones. (See "Accepting Exceptions" on page 137 for more info.)

© 2020 MARENEM

ar

These two are best friends, but it's not always easy being best friends with a superhero! A is always flying around doing superhero stuff, so r rarely gets to see him! Having a superhero as your best friend does have one perk, though. Whenever a and r do get together, a will always loan his superpowers to r so that r can see what it feels like to say HIS name! "ARRRRRRRRR!" And that's the sound they make!

art, car, hard

SECRET

© 2020 MARENEM

ACTION!!

Put muscle arms up when saying, "A gives his superpowers to r so that r can say HIS name!"

Introduce this SECRET when going to Art class for the first time. Kids should already know that "only the vowels have the power to say their names," so they should be curious why R is getting to say HIS name in "Art!"

© 2020 Marenem

al

These letters love to play with balls... ALL balls!

SECRET

Footballs, basketballs, baseballs, soccer balls, you name it!

ALL about balls, ALL the time, "ALLLLL! ALLLLL! ALLLLL!"

And that's the sound they make!

all, also, always

ACTION!!

Over-exaggerate the "AL" sound and encourage kids to come up with more kinds of balls that could be incorporated into the story.

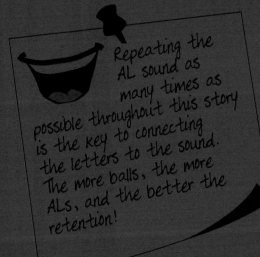

Repeating the AL sound as many times as possible throughout this story is the key to connecting the letters to the sound. The more balls, the more ALs, and the better the retention!

"Did you know that L has a twin brother, and he loves balls too, so he always tags along! You might just think you have double vision, as you'll see double L's in most words containing this SECRET!"
(all, fall, call)

© 2020 MARENEM

er / ir / ur

These friends just love to go riding in cars.

But they are terrible, awful, horrible, no-good drivers, and they always have to slam on the brakes...

"ERRRRRRRRRR!"
And that's the sound they make!

her, bird, turn

© 2020 MARENEM

 ACTION!!

Hold an imaginary steering wheel as if you're driving, and then slam on the imaginary brakes while screeching, 'ERRRRRRR!'"

Really screech out the "ERRRRR" sound while slamming down on the brake pedal!

This provides critical auditory and kinesthetic connections for easier pattern and sound retrieval.

To cement both the letters and sound to muscle-memory, recite exactly as follows: "ER, IR and UR love to go driving in cars, but they're terrible, awful, horrible, no-good drivers and they always have to slam on the brakes...ERRRRRR!"

Tell the kids that "Every now and then ER, IR and UR will invite W and OR to go for a ride in their car...and it's always a rough ride- "ERRRRR!"

That's why sometimes, WOR says "ERRRR" too!

(word, world, worm)

© 2020 MARENEM

or

SECRET

These two can't make up their minds about anything, especially about what to do when they get together to play.

They spend all of their time trying to decide, "Should we ride bikes? OR...we could go to the playground and swing? OR...we could eat cake!"

All day long, it's "OR-OR-OR!" And that's the sound they make!

for, more, corner

© 2020 MARENEM

ACTION!!

Scratch your head as if thinking over a tough decision, and becoming more and more excited with each new idea about what to do, always putting extra emphasis on the word "OR!"

Encourage students to come up with their own delicious food options, making sure to over-exaggerate the "OR" sound in-between! Just like with the AL SECRET, the repetition of the "OR" sound is key!

Tell the kids that every now and then, OR will invite W and AR over to their house to play.

But they never have much fun since OR can never decide what to do. So they all sit around saying "OR-OR-OR!"

That's why sometimes, WAR says "OR" too!

(warm, reward, quarter)

© 2020 MARENEM

au / aw

SECRET

These cute couples are head-over-heels in love, and have huge crushes on each other!

Whenever they have to stand right next to each other in a word, they get so embarrassed that they always look down and blush, saying,

"AWWWWWWWW!"
And that's the sound they make!

August, awful, saw

© 2020 MARENEM

ACTION!!

Think comic strip sweethearts, with blushing cheeks and batting eyelashes! Tilt your head to the side, your cheek touching your shoulder, eyes glancing downward toward the floor, and bat your eyelashes! Clasp your hands together, and then, as if embarrassed with an aw-shucks expression as you say, "AWWWWWWW!"

This is a great one to share on the very first day of school at Calendar Time (if starting school in August!) Kids love it, and it's the perfect way to kick off the SECRETS!

© 2020 MARENEM

ou / ow

When these tough guys get together, they play really rough and someone always gets hurt. They cry, "OWWWWWWWW!" And that's the sound they usually make!

SECRET

how, now, house, couch

But, if they ever spot SUPERHERO o flying overhead, they will stop dead in their tracks (as he's their idol!) and shout his name,

"OOOOOOOOOO!" And that's the other sound they can make!

slow, blow, though, dough

© 2020 MARENEM

ACTION!!

After telling the story, grab any part of your body as if in pain (the elbow works well!), and yell out, "OWWWW!" After a moment or two, look up and point, as if you've just spotted your favorite superhero flying through the sky, and then start shouting in your most excited voice, "O-O-O!"

The long O sound is the next-most likely "default" sound for these letters, which is why Superhero O can be seen flying overhead! So, tell kids "If the first sound doesn't work, just try the other one!" (blow, flow, know)

© 2020 MARENEM

oi / oy

SECRET

These guys love
to clown around,
bounce up and down,
and make silly sounds!

"OOY-YEE! OOY-YEE! OOY-YEE!"
And that's the sound they make!

boy, toy, soil, coin

© 2020 MARENEM

ACTION!!

Repeat the sounds, "OOY-YEE,
OOY-YEE, OOY-YEE" over and over,
exaggerating the movement of the lips
as they move back and forth for each
sound. If you do it right, you should
look pretty funny—like a clown! You can
also incorporate a bouncing motion
by bending your knees down on the
first part of the sound (OOY) and
straightening back up again for the
second part (YEE). Repeat!

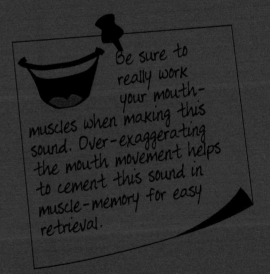

Be sure to really work your mouth-muscles when making this sound. Over-exaggerating the mouth movement helps to cement this sound in muscle-memory for easy retrieval.

© 2020 Marenem

SECRET

These two look so much like owl eyes when they get together, that they pretend to be one! "OOO-OOO!" And that's the sound they usually make!

hoot, spooky, room

Their second favorite thing to pretend to be is a pirate! They swing their arm like a hook, and in their best pirate-voice, say— "UUUHHH!"

hook, book, took

© 2020 MARENEM

ACTION!!

To make the owl sound, curl your hands like binoculars around your eyes and say "OOO-OOO!" (doing your best owl impression!).

To make the pirate sound, curl your arm at the elbow like a hook, and then swing it across your body, while saying, "UHHH!" (like in hook).

Hear and feel the difference between the "hooty" OO sound, in words like hoot and boot, and the more "guttural" OO sound, in words like book and hook. (Think a punch to the gut- "UUH!") Have kids accentuate the sound as they swing their hooked arm up!

When practicing this SECRET sound, kids should say- "OOOOOOO and "UHHHHHH!" (as they switch from owl-eyes to arm-hooks! (See ACTION CUE.)

© 2020 MARENEM

ey / ay

These dudes are just too cool! They always stick up their thumbs and say, "AAAYYY!" And that the sound they make!

SECRET

they, obey, play, say

But sometimes, ey pretends to be SUPERHERO e, and makes her sound instead (as nothing is cooler than making a superhero's sound!) "EEEEEEEE!" And that's the other sound ey can make.

key, turkey, chimney

© 2020 MARENEM

ACTION!!

Act like you're just too cool as you give a thumbs-up gesture and say, "AAAAYYYYEEEE!" (And remember to use your coolest voice!)

Let the kids know that AY is actually MUCH cooler than EY, so he can be found in a lot more words! (Helping learners realize what's most likely can give them a leg-up when spelling!)

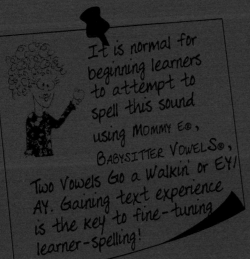

It is normal for beginning learners to attempt to spell this sound using MOMMY E®, BABYSITTER VOWELS®, Two Vowels Go a Walkin' or EY/AY. Gaining text experience is the key to fine-tuning learner-spelling!

© 2020 MARENEM

eu / ew

These prissy little girls with their pretty little curls are deathly afraid of mice!

If they ever spot one, they jump up high on their tippy-toes and scream, "EEEUUUUUUU!" And that's the sound they make!

few, chew, feud, Europe

© 2020 MARENEM

ACTION!!

The "prissier the better" when it comes to making this sound (as otherwise, it can sound like "OOOO" in hoot!)

With arms straight down against your sides and wrists-up, use your prissy-voice and squeal, "EEEUUUUUUU" as if you just spotted mice at your feet!

It's important to think "prissy" when making this sound so that it doesn't sound like the OO sound in "hoot," which is similar, but not the same. (This one has more "u" in it!)

© 2020 Marenem

qu

Q never goes anywhere without his best buddy u, and together they make one sound.

"KWUH."

SECRET

queen, quiet, quarter

ACTION!!

Students can stand with a friend, arm in arm (like best buddies) and make the "KWUH" sound together.

You will never find a Q without u right behind it, so I recommend just writing in the letter u after the Q on your alphabet display. This helps learners to visually identify their sounds as one when reading or spelling. (You can also hang the QU poster just above or in place of the letter Q in your class alphabet.)

When referencing the letter Q during reading, spelling or singing, always refer to it as "QU," so as to reinforce the two letters as one sound pattern.

To help kids remember how to properly write the lowercase "q" (with the stick on the right side), tell them that "Q always reaches back to hold hands with u!"

© 2020 MARENEM

kn / wr / mb / rh / gn

SECRET

These letters
make good
partners because
one is shy and the other is not.

That's why one always has to
speak for the other.

knee, write, thumb, rhyme, gnat

ACTION!!

A fun activity for this one (as well as for the "Two Vowels Go A-Walkin'" SECRET) is to transform your students into SECRETS by giving them cards, hats, vests, etc., with the letters on them. They can then pair up with other letters (kids) to act out the SECRETS, or even to spell entire words!

Letting your kids BECOME the letters by acting out their SECRETS is a great way to bring phonics skills to life! This helps to forge deep and personal connections to otherwise "random" letters and sounds.

It's easy to make letter vests out of brown paper grocery bags, so be sure and grab a bunch (and ask parents to do the same) the next time you go grocery shopping.

© 2020 Marenem

ce / ci / cy & ge / gi / gy

SECRET

This musical group loves to sing and clap their sounds to the "Mexican Hat Dance!"

They sing their names and then clap their hands in the air as they make their sounds!

cent, circle, bicycle
gem, giant, gym

© 2020 MARENEM

ACTION!!

Sing the letters and sounds (as shown below) to the tune of the "Mexican Hat Dance." You can search for the tune online, if unfamiliar (or on the SECRET STORIES Youtube Channel).

First, sing the letter names, and then clap twice in the air (above your shoulder) while making the sounds.

C-E C-I C-Y.....ss-ss!   ss-ss!
              (clap)   (clap)

[Sing verse 4 times]

G-E G-I G-Y.........jj-jj!   jj-jj!
              (clap)   (clap)

[Sing verse 4 times]

A Handy Spelling Trick.... The letter C makes a hard K sound before A, O, and U (cat, cop, cut) and a soft S sound before E, I, and Y. (cent, city, cycle) Likewise for G! (gas, go, gut, gem, giant, gym).

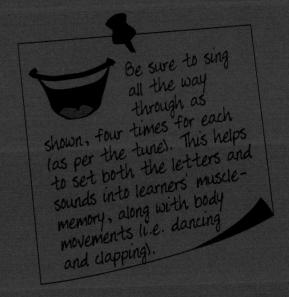

Be sure to sing all the way through as shown, four times for each (as per the tune). This helps to set both the letters and sounds into learners' muscle-memory, along with body movements (i.e. dancing and clapping).

© 2020 MARENEM

ch

These two love to ride the train down the track, chugging along as they go-

SECRET

"CH-CH-CH-CH!
CH-CH-CH-CH!
CH-CH-CH-CH!"

And that's the sound they make!
church, chin, chew

But sometimes they pretend to be the train conductor, and like to make his hard C (or K) sound instead!
choir, school, schedule

© 2020 Marenem

ACTION!!

Basically you want to act like a train going down the track, with arms bent at the elbows and moving in a circular motion. (Think old-fashioned "choo-choo" trains as they chug along the tracks!)

Then pretend to be the train conductor, waiving your imaginary conductor's cap as the train passes by!

Remember to make only the "CH" sound (and not the old standard, "Chugga-Chugga-Choo-Choo") sound, as the latter will confuse learners by introducing additional and unnecessary sounds. Simply repeat the "CH" sound four times in succession (as shown) to solidify it in learners' muscle-memory.

© 2020 MARENEM

ph

These two are very immature, and when they get together, they love to make phoney phone calls!

Their favorite phoney phone call to make is to pretend to be Mr. F, and say—

"FFFFF! FFFFF! FFFFF!"

And then they hang up really fast! And that's the sound they make.

phone, dolphin, trophy

© 2020 MARENEM

ACTION!!

Pretend to hold an imaginary phone and say, "FFFFF! FFFFF! FFFFF!" (and then hang up really fast!).

It might help to explain to students what a phoney phone call actually is before telling this story. (Just try not to give them any ideas!)

sh

This studious pair spends most of their time at the library reading books, but they can't concentrate when it's noisy, and so they are always reminding everyone to be quiet.

SECRET

They say, "SHHHHHHHHH!"
And that's the sound they make!

she, show, wish

ACTION!!

Put finger to lips and make the "SHHHHHHHHH" sound very quietly.

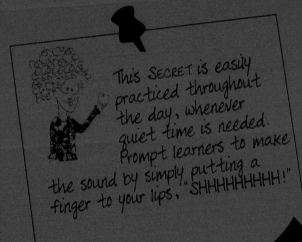

This SECRET is easily practiced throughout the day, whenever quiet time is needed. Prompt learners to make the sound by simply putting a finger to your lips, "SHHHHHHHHH!"

© 2020 MARENEM

th

These two should never be together EVER!! But pick up any book, and turn to any page, and guess who you see, side-by-side? That's right, t and h! And every time they're together, they always stick out their tongues and say,

"THHHHHHHHHHHHHHHHHHH!"

And that's the sound they make!

the, with, this

© 2020 MARENEM

ACTION!!

Make your brattiest face and stick your tongue out as far as you can to make the "THHHHHHHHH" sound.

This SECRET does not distinguish between the "voiced" TH sound (as in the word "this") and the "unvoiced" TH sound (as in the word "thin"). The reason being, it's just not necessary, as once kids know to stick their tongues out, and are able to decode the rest of the word, most can easily make the necessary sound adjustment.

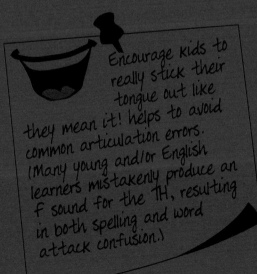

Encourage kids to really stick their tongue out like they mean it! helps to avoid common articulation errors. (Many young and/or English learners mistakenly produce an f sound for the TH, resulting in both spelling and word attack confusion.)

© 2020 MARENEM

wh

These guys are always worn out from playing so hard and so long all day.

They're always out-of-breath and panting.

"WHHHHHH! WHHHHHH! WHHHHHH!" And that's the sound they make!

why, what, when

ACTION!!

Do your best imitation of having just run a mile at top-speed! Let your arms hang down to your sides, lean over slightly (as if overtaken by total exhaustion!) and then, between big huffy breaths and in your best "almost-ready-to-fall-over-and-die voice," puff-out a, "WHHHHHH! WHHHHHH! WHHHHHH!"

This sound should be made entirely on the breath, and without any vocal chord involvement/ vibration.

© 2020 Marenem

gh

SECRET

When g and h are at the BEGINNING of a word, they love being the line leaders. They shout,"Good! This is great! We get to go first!" "GUH-GUH-GUH!" (Hard G sound)
    ghost, ghastly, ghoul

When they are in the MIDDLE of a word, surrounded by other letters, they're too afraid to talk at all, so they stay silent.
    eight,thought,sight

When they're at the END of a word, they always complain "We're so far away! This is taking forever! We should be first!" "FFFFF-FFFFF-FFFFF" (F sound)
    rough, enough, tough

© 2020 MARENEM

ACTION!!

Pretend to be gh when they're the line leader! In your most excited voice (and exaggerating all of the hard G sounds) say, "Good, good, good! This is great! We get to go first!"

Pretend to be gh when in the middle and afraid of all the other letters. Just cover your mouth as if you're too afraid to speak, saying NOTHING!

Pretend to be gh at the end of a very long line, and in your most annoyed and irritated voice, start complaining, "Man, we're so far away! It's going to take forever to get to the front!" making sure to exaggerate the F sounds.

Whenever Superhero I is right in front of GH in a word he will use his superpowers to protect them (since they're so scared!) How many words can you find where I is using his super powers to make GH feel safe? (right, light, fight)

When GH isn't making the sound that it should (based on its position in a word), it just makes one of the other two sounds, instead. So try its MOST likely sound first, and then one of the other two if needed. (tough, though)

© 2020 MARENEM

ing / ang / ong / ung /ink / ank / onk / unk

ING—ANG—ONG—UNG...
make the sounds of
bells rung.

SECRET

INK—ANK—ONK—UNK...
make the sounds of bells that
clunk!"

"INGGG—ANGGG—ONGGG—UNGGG"

"INK—ANK—ONK—UNK"

And those are the sounds that they
make!

sing, sang, song, sung

sink, sank, honk, chunk

© 2020 MARENEM

ACTION!!

Think a chiming clock (but without the "D" sound at the beginning) as you use say "INGGG-ANGGG-ONGGG-UNGGG" in your best sing-songy voice! Then speak (in your "clunkiest" voice) "INK-ANK-ONK-UNK," with a hard "K" sound at the end.

Use a "sing-songy" voice when telling this story—especially when making the sounds of ING, ANG, ONG, and UNG. This will help solidify the sounds in learners' muscle-memory for easier retrieval. Likewise, exaggerate the hard K sound at the end of INK, ANK, ONK and UNK for the same reason.

Tell the kids that the reason INK, ANK, ONK and UNK no longer ring (like ING, ANG, ONG and UNG) is because they fell and broke. (That's why they sound so "clunky!")

© 2020 MARENEM

ed

E and d are big fans of SNEAKY Y®! They love that he can make the sounds of OTHER letters, and they want to be just like him!

So even though their name is Ed, they will sometimes make the D or T sounds, instead!

"ED-DUH-TUH!"

And those are are the sounds they can make!

waited, played, skipped

© 2020 MARENEM

ACTION!!

Start with your hands clasped together and bent at the elbows in front of your chest, as you say "ED." Then, let your left arm fall to the left side as you say "DUH," and your right arm fall to the right side as you say "TUH."

E and D are SNEAKY Y®'s biggest fans, which is why they carry his picture around with them everywhere they go!

© 2020 MARENEM

tion / sion / ation

ACTION!!

SECRET

These friends remember how badly their other friends drive, so they don't have cars. Instead, they prefer to take the train.

But they get bored waiting around the station, so to help pass the time, they make up little chants to say while they're waiting! (See "Action" cue.)

question, expression, transportation

© 2020 MARENEM

Use a locomotive, or "choo-choo-train" (i.e. circular, back-and-forth) arm motion while repeating the following rhythmic chant with the letter names, followed by the sounds. This chant should be spoken "in-time" with the arm motion, and with added emphasis on the first letter in each set.

SAY capital letters by NAME followed by "shun" sound.

T-I-O-N shuuun!   T-I-O-N shuuuun!
S-I-O-N shuuun!   S-I-O-N shuuuun!

Use superhero arms for SUPERHERO A sounds!

Ayye shuuun!   Ayye shuuun!
A   TION   A   TION

Note: These last two lines are a little bit different, as you chant SOUNDS only and then the LETTERS only, 2x each.

Watch this one in action on the Secret Stories® YouTube Channel. Click the "Learn More" tab on our website, and then select "Videos" to find the channel link.

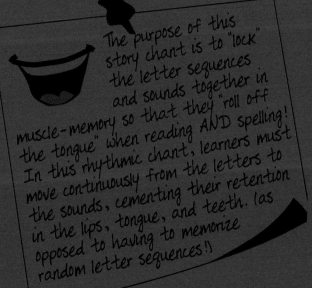

The purpose of this story chant is to "lock" the letter sequences and sounds together in muscle-memory so that they "roll off the tongue" when reading AND spelling! In this rhythmic chant, learners must move continuously from the letters to the sounds, cementing their retention in the lips, tongue, and teeth. (as opposed to having to memorize random letter sequences!)

Superhero A is their favorite superhero. That's why they made a special chant with her name at the front!

© 2020 MARENEM

ion

These letters adore staying up late at night to read their favorite book (SECRET STORIES® of course!). Their late night reading often leaves them extremely tired in the morning, making it very hard to get up and out of bed! They just can't seem to stop yawning. "YUUUUHHHNN!" (It sounds almost like a yawn, but not quite!)

And that's the sound they make!

opinion, onion, million

© 2020 MARENEM

As if just waking up, stretch arms overhead in a yawning motion and make the sound, "YUUUUHHHNN!" (Almost like "YAWN" but not quite!).

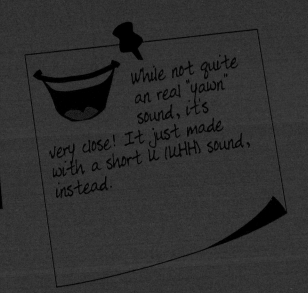

While not quite an real "yawn" sound, it's very close! It just made with a short u (UHH) sound, instead.

© 2020 MARENEM

ie

Superhero e is not at all happy with Superhero i. Not only did he keep one of her capes that he found, but whenever they take walks together, he wants to do ALL the talking! So she came up with a plan. She brings cookies for him to eat on their walks so his mouth is too full to talk. That way, SHE gets to talk and say HER name, instead! "EEEEEEEEEE!" And that's the sound they usually make!

cookie, believe, field

But sometimes, e runs out of cookies, so i gets to say HIS name, instead! "IIIIIIIII!" And that's the other sound they can make.

lie, cries, pie

© 2020 MARENEM

ACTION!!

Pair kids up as Superhero i and Superhero e. Then let Superhero e pretend to stuff imaginary (or real!) cookies in Superhero i's mouth so he can't talk, while Superhero e happily makes her sound.

This could be why Superhero I's suit is getting tight and he does all those exercises! He's been taking too many walks with Superhero E (and eating too many cookies!)

© 2020 MARENEM

ous

ACTION!!

As everyone knows, when three friends play together, it's only a matter of time before one is left out.

SECRET

When o, u and s play together, it's always poor little o who's left out of the fun, crying his eyes out, and unable to talk. That's why when o, u and s get together, it's just "US-US-US!"

And that's the sound they make!

curious, serious, famous

© 2020 MARENEM

Assign each of the three letters above to three students who will dramatize poor little o being sad and left out, while u and s happily chirp out, "US-US-US!" with arms wrapped around each other, as if they are best friends for life!

Let muscle-memory guide learners from the symbols to the sound for the three letters in this sequence. To do this, have kids retell the story exactly as follows: "When O, u, and S get together, it's just 'US!'"

© 2020 Marenem

Supersonic Blends

ACTION!!

SECRET

These letters have no SECRETS. They just make their regular sounds, only "smushed" together!

That's because they've been left in the blender a bit too long, being tossed, turned, and squished every which way.

When they were finally splattered out, they got stuck together and now their sounds are combined!

blend, drive, slip, play, sweep

© 2020 MARENEM

bl, br, cl, cr, dr, fl, fr, gl, gr, pl, pr, sc, sk, sl, sm, sn, sp, st, sw, tr, tw, scr, spl, spr, str

Assign each student a different letter, call out a blend sound (saying just the sound, not the letters) and see how fast the correct pair can come together. Students can also sort themselves into blends, and even SECRETS, as they pull together to make words!

black, brush, clown, drive, flower, frown, glow, growl, please, pretty, scoot, skip, slide, smell, snow, speak, stay, sweep, tree, tweet, scratch, splash, spray, stress

Remember to alternate blend practice by moving from "sound to symbol" and "symbol to sound." Doing so mimics the decoding and encoding processes and increases automaticity for reading and writing. (See Music Download Tracks 15-18 for more. Code on the back cover.)

Display the blender with blend droplets scattered around it for hands-on play and practice. (Use Velcro dots to "stick" the blends all around the blender for fun practice! You can also add "cut-outs" of individual letters that students can use to make words. (Reproducible student copies can be found on page 172.)

© 2020 Marenem

3 Why *Secret Stories*® Work

The Paradigm Shift

Reading isn't math— despite how we might teach them. Kindergartners are not expected to add or subtract numbers before first learning how to identify them, nor are second graders ever called upon to perform long division before learning how to multiply. When teaching math, it makes sense to approach the material in a linear fashion, with kindergarten focusing on number sense, first grade on addition and subtraction, second grade on multiplication and simple division, etc. Not so when teaching reading, as learners will naturally encounter *all* of the letters and sound patterns from the very beginning, and in no particular order. It is impossible to shield early grade students from advanced phonics patterns, regardless of the text level. Thus, my mantra that "*t* is no more or less important than *th!*"

When you tell your students the story about *au / aw* having crushes on each other, you haven't asked them to memorize anything. You told them a story; that is, you *gave* them a skill— which is a very different thing from *teaching* it. And as you continue to tell them the stories, you're simply giving them all access to these skills. A child at a buffet may only be interested in eating mashed potatoes, but he can still identify where the pot roast, ice cream, salad, and beverages are. And while Johnny may have no current need or interest in any of those things, Max wants to eat everything. Adelia is happy choosing two or three things, but her curiosity to try a few new dishes is spurred on by watching Max devour everything in sight.

The point of the buffet analogy is that whether the students know what to do with the code or not, they all know the Secrets— what they are, what they look like, and what they say. Secret

DEEP LEARNING

"Deep learning provides a context for understanding, in which passion and insatiable curiosity flourish– weaving a virtual tapestry of connections that grounds one's learning in the roots of personal meaning and purpose."

–Stephanie Pace Marshall

What about Letter-of-the-Week?

Every letter, every sound, every day! This is the *Secret Stories*® motto! Just think about all the words that learners encounter throughout the day. Each and every one provides a potential springboard into the study of all of the letters and sounds—and most importantly, into the world of *Secret Stories*® — where a *t* is no more or less important than a *th*.

And besides, you're not going to *teach* all the letters and sounds, you're going to *give* them via muscle-memory (for the individual letters) or non-consciously, via the affective learning domain.

Stories® gives every learner access to the *whole* code, not just bits and pieces to those who are deemed "ready." This is what teaching through the brain's backdoor is all about. The social-emotive, or affective learning networks that are located in the back area of the brain process emotions that we never have to teach our students, for they innately know what joy, excitement, embarrassment, etc. feel like. They also know what happens if they don't listen to Mommy, or if two overly active kids sit next to each other in class (*t* and *h* are just like those two kids, by the way). Anchoring ideas about text to this center of the brain has just tricked the brain into receiving information that otherwise it would not have gotten. Memorizing sight words never activates this part of the brain because it relies on the front parts of the brain that aren't as well developed, especially in early and struggling learners.

It is within this buffet-style approach to phonics instruction that learners become their own gatekeepers in the acquisition of these critical skills. In other words, learners can know where all of the types of food on a buffet are located and how to get a hold of them, even if they only want one thing. The same is true for all of the letters and sounds explained by the SECRETS. They know where everything is, what it looks like, and what it's for (that is, where the poster is, what the pattern looks like, what sound it makes)— they just may not have any personal use for it yet. We've given them access to all of the pieces, but allowed them the space to wait until they have a hankering for them before plugging them in. In essence, they become their own gatekeepers, driven by their own curiosity to know more grown-up SECRETS.

That driving curiosity and intrigue of learning what grown-ups know about reading and writing completely fascinates them. Their natural curiosity here is key to making them want to learn, because brain-based instruction depends on their internal motivation to want to know. As even the youngest learners realize they can easily spot the SECRETS hidden within words, they'll want to know more and more, creating that push and pull cyclical process that ultimately places them into the driver's seat of their own instruction.

DRIVE LEARNING WITH CURIOSITY AND THE NON-CONSCIOUS MIND

Researchers are continually updating how important curiosity is for sparking learning. Studies suggest that our brain chemistry actually changes when we become curious, and those changes help us better learn and retain information. They have noted that the brain reacts well to receiving rewards (by releasing dopamine), and when learning is linked to something it finds intrinsically rewarding it is enhanced. So when a child wants to learn a SECRET, and views that as a reward, you've created a strong pathway to learning by giving it to him.

Research shows that more than 99 percent of learning occurs at the non-conscious level, which means visual cues, sounds, and experiences all turn us into veritable walking, talking, sponges. Learning is fluid and effortless at this level— occurring naturally, regardless of socio-economic status, language background, skill, ability, or experience level— and with no differentiation of instruction required. So sharing SECRET STORIES® with your classroom literally levels the playing field and allows all learners to access the skills they'll need to advance and progress.

BACKDOOR

Skill acquisition at the non-conscious level is akin to slipping in the brain's backdoor– which is always wide open and easily accessible.

Alternatively, conscious learning— the predominant means through which learners acquire skills in school— is far from fluid, and proves anything but effortless, especially for early grade and struggling learners. It requires that students be not only well prepared and attentive, but put forth both a determined and directed effort as well. The conscious level of learning also requires that students be developmentally, or cognitively ready to learn, and that the necessary foundation has been laid for it.

What's important to realize is that conscious learning relies upon early learners' slower to develop, higher-level processing capability in the executive functioning center, located at the front area of the brain. In sharp contrast, non-conscious learning occurs in the more rapidly developing, social-emotive centers, or affective learning domain, which is located in the rear, and more primitive area of the brain.

Because our brains develop from back to front, by simply wrapping up skill content in a social-emotive disguise, we are able to effectively bypass areas of early learner-weakness and tap into alternate areas of strength. No longer must early grade teachers (or those working with struggling, upper grade learners) be slaves to their developmental or cognitive readiness, as now we can *give* them the skills, rather than *teach* them.

The difference between cognitive processing and affective learning is most easily demonstrated by a typical student's response to the following question, "What did you learn in school today?" Prompting a common answer, "Nothing...." This common exchange is in great contrast to the virtual diatribe likely to erupt upon asking that same student what happened in their classroom instead.

> "Right before lunch Suzy got sent to the principal's office for hitting Marcus in line. He's the kid who can't eat peanuts and speaks Portuguese, so he always has to stand right behind the line leader so the teacher can keep him away from peanuts. Hmmm... I wonder what would happen to him if he ever did get one. Anyway, Suzy already got sent to the principal like a *million* times this week already.... so she acted like she didn't care.... but I could tell she did, cause her face was really red and she looked ready to cry... Anyway, after Suzy was gone, Marcus started to get really excited..... I could tell because he was jumping up and down. I think he thought that *he* would get to take Suzy's assigned job as line-leader....but I knew he wouldn't, 'cause I remembered he had gotten a time-out yesterday..... and that meant Jerry would get to be next. I think Jerry already figured that out too, cause I noticed him smiling kinda funny when he saw Marcus dancing around, all happy and everything.... Oh! And guess *who* gets to be

the line-leader if Jerry goes to time-out….. *me*!!! But I doubt that'll ever happen…. Jerry's so quiet…. he *never* gets in trouble... well, except for that one time at the beginning of the year when……"

And on and on it goes...the learner enthusiastically expounding in great detail about the social-emotive "goings-on" within his classroom, both analyzing and hypothesizing as he goes. Non-conscious learning has rendered him a virtual expert— empowering him to think at a higher level, as he critically analyzes and effectively diagnoses who the line leader should be and why.

Herein lies the awesome power of the non-conscious mind— regardless of an identified need or label— be it: LD, ESL, SPED, ADD, AG, EH, or any other of the countless varieties of diagnosable-acronyms— such content becomes deeply embedded within the learner, established through personal and meaningful connections to that which he was already familiar— a context which immediately triggers non-conscious learning to occur. Learners are highly capable of both critically analyzing and diagnostically assessing all of the information they acquire in this way. Even still, traditional education and instruction are centered on that of conscious learning— consisting of mostly rapid, passive, and often superficial acquisition of random, disembodied information— and nowhere is this more true than in the area of literacy skill instruction.

Current brain research proves that it is well within our capabilities, as educators, to harness this tremendous power of non-conscious learning, and transfer those most critical, complex, and practice-based skills to the easily accessible, non-conscious realm. The secret to successfully transferring abstract, skill-

A PLAYGROUND FOR CRITICAL THINKING

With knowledge of the *SECRET STORIES®*, daily reading and writing can become a virtual playground for critical thinking.

based content from that which must be consciously learned, to that which can be non-consciously acquired, lies within a very specific instructional context— one in which learners are engaged in what researchers refer to as deep learning. A learner that is engaged in deep learning is both active and reflective. "Deep learning provides learners with a context for understanding in which passion and insatiable curiosity flourish— weaving a virtual tapestry of connections that grounds one's learning in the roots of personal meaning and purpose."

It is only by embedding these seemingly random and abstract phonemic skills within real-life contexts that they may be naturally acquired through non-conscious learning. As all substitute teachers know, students can be quite assertive, at times, in their attempts to provide what they deem as relevant information about their classroom— often giving far more than the substitute needs, or even wants, to know. Even learners who speak little-to-no English will find a way to share— if only by way of hand-gesturing. Not a single learner in the room can forgo the temptation to explain all of the many reasons why Jimmy and Johnny can't sit together, or why Emma can't eat a peanut, each involving a lengthy and detailed description of past incidents that had occurred whenever this rule was not followed.

We can tap into these same learning channels by embedding complex phonemic skill content within familiar scenarios and learner experiences, so as to be equally easy and effortless to acquire. This means that the same neural pathways Johnny uses to tell the substitute teacher about who can't sit together in class are utilized to retrieve abstract phonics patterns and sounds. This is because both sets of information now reside in the same area within the brain— which is the affective domain.

CHEATING THE BRAIN

The same neural pathways used to tell the substitute who can't sit together in class are used to retrieve complex phonemic patterns and sounds.

CHANGE THE FACTS

One of my favorite quotes is, "If the facts don't fit the theory, change the facts!" (popularly credited to Albert Einstein). It is a fact there is no inherent meaning in phonics with regard to the many different sounds that letters make, and it is also a fact that without meaningful explanations to provide our students about why the letters actually do what they do, reading is destined to remain a constant struggle for learners, as well as teachers. But, if we follow the logic of Einstein, then the solution to this problem is quite simple. We simply change the facts. (*Poof!* I just did it.)

LEVELING THE PLAYING FIELD

With meaning comes genuine understanding, through which logical deductions can easily be made.

Now everything makes perfect sense, as there are perfectly logical explanations *why* letters make the sounds that they do. It's because they're in love like *au* and *aw*, or sneaky like *y*, or maybe they are just really bad drivers like *er, ir* and *ur*. But whatever they are, they do what they do for a reason.

Changing the facts makes learning to read (and teaching it) simple. No more having to say, "It just is, it just does, you'll just have to remember." Now we can just tell them *why*. The SECRET STORIES® explain why the letters are who they are and say what they do instead of merely providing learners with repetitive skill practice. By taking advantage of the learning loopholes rooted in our brain's own neural plasticity, we can just *give* learners all of the skills they need, and they can just *take* them. Now that just makes sense— and how often can we say that in reading?

Accepting Exceptions

When it comes to phonics we don't normally consider thinking outside the box. What's important to keep in mind when thinking about exceptions is that learners cannot think outside of the box until they first understand what's in it. Put yet, another way, "You can't apply critical thought to something over which you have only a basic understanding" (Albert Einstein). This quote provides the greatest insight into why we have traditionally viewed exceptions as impossible to decode, especially for beginning readers.

The primary (and really only) goal of the *Secret Stories*® is to help beginning readers quickly attain a functional, yet comprehensive, skill set so as to effectively work their way through unfamiliar text— including exceptions— from the earliest possible grade level. Research shows that experience is by far, the best teacher. However, the value of that experience that learners actually take away is based on how many tools they bring to the table with which to partake in it. The *Secret Stories*® are the tools that learners bring to the table to ensure the most value from their daily text experiences.

After reading through the Classified *Secret Stories*® section, you can see that not all sounds have a SECRET. And not every SECRET explains all possible sounds. The standard used in creating the *Secret Stories*® was based upon whether or not a letter or phonics pattern occurs on a frequent enough basis to require an explanation. For the purposes of the *Secret Stories*® the magic number was generally five times or more. If a sound shows up in five or more words that students are likely to encounter, then I created a SECRET that equips them to handle it. This method provides the foundation for this common sense approach to phonics.

BOTTOM LINE

The more tools learners bring to the reading and writing table, the more value they take away.

This means that when initially looking at the *Secret Stories*® you might find yourself wondering about all the exceptions to the rules (or the Secrets) that exist, which is completely okay. Exceptions are generally defined as words in which a letter or letters aren't making the sound or sounds that they should, based on phonetic rules in English. You may even be asking yourself how the *Secret Stories*®, or even phonics in general, could even work, given all of the exceptions in the English language. The answer is simple. Once learners know what's in the box (that is, all possible sound "behaviors" for the letters) then it's not that hard to think outside of it (that is, deduce their most likely and next most likely sounds).

I have been asked before why certain sound patterns don't have Secrets. I go back to the rule that a sound needs to happen frequently enough to merit explanation, and then explain that too many Secrets will spoil the stew. Requiring readers to learn too many Secrets would lessen the overall effectiveness of the *Secret Stories*® as a whole. Creating Secrets to account for sound patterns not critical to learners' success in reading is the equivalent of having "too many cooks in the kitchen," and would only thwart learners in their ability to more rapidly acquire the comprehensive base of skills (Secrets) they do need. In other words, too many Secrets would only lessen the effectiveness of the *Secret Stories*® as a whole. Streamlining and consolidating the phonics rules of our language reinforces and further solidifies reading and writing skill proficiency.

LETTERS DON'T GO BONKERS!

Have you ever heard an *a* sound like a *zzzzzzz*? I didn't think so! Letters don't go bonkers – they just make their next most likely sounds.

Scenario-based Training (or SBT, as it is commonly referred to by the military when used to train inexperienced soldiers) dictates that you can immediately rule out unlikely and impossible situations. Your students will know that even if a letter isn't behaving properly, there are only so many things it can do. An *a* can't start sounding like a *k*, for example. Letters can't just make any old sound that they please, and that is exactly what I tell students when we talk about letters and sounds that don't appear to make sense. Even when they aren't doing what they're supposed to, the letters haven't gone completely crazy. If Mom isn't sitting where they think she should be, they know to check the living room and then her bedroom. They already know and understand that she isn't hiding in the cupboards above the kitchen sink! Letters are the same exact way, and by helping them to see letters and sounds the way they see and understand themselves and the world around them, they can make sense of text with a similar familiarity. So even in the world of exceptions, the letters and sounds still play by the rules to a degree.

SECRET STORIES® equips learners to decipher letters and letter patterns using the most likely sound, and then to immediately move to the next most likely sound if that doesn't work, and so on, establishing a hierarchy of likelihood within learners for the most effective decision making when working with unfamiliar text. Tackling text in this way promotes the flexible thinking learners need to accept and minimize the exceptions.

A letter or letter pattern is said to be doing what it should when it is making its most likely sound, based on the SECRET. A letter or letter pattern not doing what it should implies that it is making a less likely, or alternative, sound. An example of a word not following the rules is have. (See page 140, "Conversation: Next Most Likely Sounds" for what to say to the kids in this scenario.)

Think about a medical student studying to become a general practitioner. She is not required to learn about every rare disease that exists, but she will learn to check the most likely things first to figure out what's happening with her patient. It would not be the most effective use of her time to focus on cases she very well may

Conversation: Next Most Likely Sounds

Student conversation for the word _have_.

Student: Hey, how come the letter _a_ isn't saying its name like it's supposed to?

Teacher: Because letters are just like kids and don't always do what they should! But that's okay. What else could the _a_ say?

S: Well… it's supposed to say _aaayyyy_ because MOMMY E® is there!

T: Johnny, let me ask you a question. Where should you be right now?

S: At my desk.

T: But you're not. You're at my desk… which is fine, as I know it's the next most likely place to find you. Can you guess where the third most likely is that I would go to look for you if you weren't at your desk or at mine? The bathroom, because that's another one of your favorite spots! Now, I would never think to look for you inside the cabinet, because that just wouldn't make sense. You see, letters are just like you, especially the vowels. They simply do what they're perfectly capable of doing anyway— it just might be the _next_ most likely thing. So Johnny, what else can the _a_ say?

S: Well, it could say _aaaaaaa_, but it's not supposed to!

T: I know, but again, where are _you_ supposed to be right now?

S: At my seat.

T: Exactly! So what else could _a_ say?

S: _aaaaaa…_

T: Well let's try that sound and see if it works.

S: _Hhhh-aaa-vvv._

T: Now that wasn't so hard, was it? You see, sometimes even mommies are just too tired to make kids do what they should, like the MOMMY E® in the word _have_.

never see. The same is true for your students as you help them to become good word doctors by familiarizing them first with the most common sound patterns they are likely to experience in text. Just like the medical student must know how to identify and treat the most likely emergency room scenarios before starting an ER rotation, our students must have an equally comprehensive, and yet bare-bones skill-set. Those basic skills are what allow the medical student to effectively assess what's most likely wrong with a patient, and the experience of diagnosing patients is what fine-tunes and extends her functional level of skill from basic to expert. And the same is true for our inexperienced readers.

Now, every good word doctor knows that the vowels (*a, e, i, o,* and *u*) are the eyes, ears, nose, and throat of a word. They are the first thing to check when having trouble sounding out a word, because vowels are the best windows into what is most likely going wrong inside a word. Helping learners identify the need to roll up those sleeves and dig into solving the problem of something that does not always look, act, or even work the way it should is an incredible gift. You are honing their ability to critically analyze and problem-solve— you're teaching them how to think! You have empowered them to not just run away from a problem they think unsolvable, but to use the tools they have to work through it and figure it out. The SECRET STORIES® are those tools.

Before learners can start thinking like doctors and learn how to diagnose words, they must build up their experience with text. More importantly, though, is that they need to have a comprehensive enough skill-base so they're capable of getting this experience. Once they have this base level achieved, they can start fine-tuning their work and concentrate on skills like spelling and reading aloud fluently and with inflection.

EXPERIENCE IS THE BEST TEACHER

The SECRET STORIES® equip beginning readers with a functional skill base, which allows them to more quickly acquire experience with text. Without this functional level of skill ability, learners are capable only of gaining *exposure* to text– which is far less valuable than *experience*.

Word Doctor Diagnosis

"I was trying to read the word July on the calendar, and at first I didn't recognize the SNEAKY Y™ at the end, so I sounded it out making y's regular sound. When that didn't work, I realized that he was being sneaky, and would be making either his e or his i sound. So first, I tried the e sound, but I got the word Jul-EE and I knew that wasn't right, 'cause there's no month that's called Jul-EE! So then I tried the i sound, Jul-I, and guess what? I got it! Without anybody's help, I got the word! It was July!"

The more you weave the SECRET STORIES® through all aspects of your instructional day, the stronger these skills become and the faster your students will begin to sharpen their "specialty" skills.

When assessing which exceptions are figure-out-able, you have the option to send a word to Word Jail or to keep working on it. Words that are not figure-out-able are immediately sentenced to serve time in our "word jail," acting as a constant reminder of our need to memorize what they look like, so "they never get by us again!"

FIGURE-OUT-ABLE

Figure-out-able *adj.* / fig•ure•OUT•a•ble:

1. A word that can be sounded out, despite some letters not making the sounds that they should

You will often notice words that learners could, for the most part sound out, but once they do, they will undoubtedly end up with an awkward pronunciation. When this happens have faith and hold off on throwing them into word jail, as most times, they are still figure-out-able. Give the learners a chance to see what they and a little reading elbow grease can come up with. Do not immediately jump to their rescue. Instead, give them an opportunity to play with those sounds a little bit first. Sometimes just bending (making small adjustments) the sound of a vowel is enough to help learners hear the word. Most often, there will be enough letters that *are* making their correct sounds for learners to come close enough to get the word.

WHAT ABOUT SIGHT WORDS?

Teaching students to memorize their lists of sight words is an age-old tradition that primary grade teachers often rely upon because students haven't yet accumulated all of the skills they need to actually *read* most words. In this context, sight word reliance is understandable, particularly given the traditional scope and sequence of literacy skill instruction—whereby beginning learners must wait until the end of second grade before gaining access to the entire reading code. This extended acquisition time is due to the inherent complexities of phonics skill instruction, paired with the broad range of early learners' developmental and cognitive readiness capabilities. However, when learners are able to access these same skills— shared as SECRETS— by way of the brain's backdoor (social emotive/affective connections) instead of the traditional "front" (abstract skill processing) acquisition is immediate and application, instant.

Research shows that teaching kids to sound out words sparks more optimal brain circuitry than instructing them to memorize them. In other words, don't waste time teaching kids to memorize words that they could actually *read*. Students who know the SECRETS are easily able to read almost all of the most common Dolch and Fry Sight Words— even in kindergarten. Teaching students to sound out *a-n-d* sparks more optimal brain circuitry than instructing them to memorize the word *and*. Furthermore, studies found that these teaching induced differences show up even on future encounters with the word.

Stanford-based research has now confirmed that beginning readers who focus on letter-sound relationships (phonics) instead of trying to learn whole words have increased activity in the area of their brains best wired for reading. In other words, you'll see more optimal brain circuitry when students sound out a word like *yellow* instead of simply trying to memorize it. The goal of the *Secret Stories*® is to share enough strategies for reading that memorization becomes a last resort.

However, memorization becomes the only option for students who don't know the Secrets because they won't know all of the phonics patterns until the end of second grade. Plus, there is a strong belief among educators that young readers will be able to recognize sight words faster than they can read them. Our job is not to train actors to memorize scripts. Our job is to teach learners how to read, and short, simple sight words provide both frequent and invaluable opportunities for beginning readers to stretch and flex their burgeoning reading muscles. Doing so will ultimately help fluency and reading speed, not hinder it.

OUTLAW WORDS

Word Jail is the place for any word that we have deemed *un-figure-out-able*. Check out the video "Sight Words go to Jail" on *Secret Stories*® YouTube channel to see what this looks like.

Students who know the Secrets know what's in the box. They are now empowered to more easily navigate those so-called exceptions when working with text. They readily apply what they know to be the most likely sound scenarios to the letter(s) they want to figure out, and when they encounter a word that isn't making its most likely sound, they move to the next most likely sound, and so on. If they still can't figure out a word, despite all of the Secrets they know, we call it an "outlaw word" and they can send it to word jail. Only then do we rely on memorization, as these are the words that we are powerless against (which is not something good word doctors like to admit). In this way the word jail becomes our last resort.

Outlaws And Word Jail

Although you may opt to sentence some figure-out-able words to some jail time due to ongoing difficulty with spelling in later grades, most often in kindergarten and first grade, absolute accuracy in spelling is not an immediate concern. Rather, the emphasis is on functional spelling, meaning that the learner can read what they've written and move forward with their story. Some words will get spelled using proper choices, as opposed to right ones. A good example of what would be considered a proper choice is the word *bird*. A learner who knows the Secrets may initially attempt to spell it *b-u-r-d*, especially if their experience with text is minimal. But as their experience as readers increases, so will their spelling accuracy. These incidental spelling errors are naturally fine-tuned through the process of daily interaction with text (that is, reading and writing, which the learner can and will do only if they possess the skills they need to do it).

It may be beneficial in early grades to delay posting the word jail until learners have become more familiar with the *Secret Stories*® and have begun using them with some level of consistency. Remember, the exceptions are best served after the Secrets so that learners can have a grasp of the rules before we ask them to recognize words that break them.

Once the little learners have gained a bit of experience they should have no trouble whatsoever recognizing true outlaw words when they see them. If you teach at a grade level that engages in weekly spelling exams, I highly recommend you provide a bonus word section, made up of two or three of the most recently captured outlaw words.

WORD DOCTOR VS. WORD WARDEN

Encourage students to become word *doctors, not* word *wardens*! Neural research shows that sounding out words provides learners far more brain-bang for their instructional-buck than memorizing words by sight.

It is important to remember that at the earliest grade levels, equipping learners with a functional ability to both read and write is the primary goal. Possessing at least a functional ability when working with text, ensures that they will be capable of gaining the experience necessary to further build upon their current level of skill.

And so, when making the final determinations as to whether or not to lock up a word for good, just remember that the learner's ability to read it is far more important than their ability to spell it, particularly at the early grade levels. Using this as your guide, decide for yourself what will best meet the needs of your students with regard to which words to lock up and which to set free.

BOTTOM LINE

There are only two letters in the word *of* and neither one is making the sound that it should, which is why it cannot be rehabilitated, but must be memorized instead.

Using the "mug shot cards" (provided in the back of this book), write down any words that students encounter during reading, writing, or discussion activities that can't be easily figured out with the SECRETS. These words should be immediately detained in the word jail. You should make several copies of these outlaw word mug shots and keep them by your word jail so that words may be immediately captured for display and reference as learners discover them in text.

Once an outlaw word has been successfully identified (captured) in text, it must then be booked and processed, meaning that we will take its picture (write it down) and throw it in jail (mount it on our word jail) so that we can remember what it looks like and it doesn't ever get by us again (catch us by surprise in future reading and writing).

MAJOR OFFENDERS

This group will make up 90 percent of your prison population. These are the worst of the outlaws words, the most egregious offenders of the rules of our language that simply cannot be trusted. They must be captured and sent to jail (memorized) as they cannot be rehabilitated. In this way, we will be able to remember how they look so that they don't get by us (in our reading, writing, or spelling) again.

The good news is that these are the only words that must be memorized. Words that fall into the major offender, or outlaw, category are almost always either one syllable, high-frequency, sight words, or, words that were originally derived from other languages that follow the rules of their native language, not English (words with origins outside of English include *pizza, armoire, buffet,* etc.). As a result, these words possess the power to render our most effective and even most secret reading strategies virtually useless.

The one syllable, high-frequency, sight words have earned their status as major offenders due to their diminutive size leaving us so little to work with as if even only one letter doesn't do what it should, that's enough to make the entire word impossible to sound out.

MOST WANTED

The most egregious offenders are non-decodable, one-syllable sight words such as: *of, do, what, want, could, would, should, there, their,* etc. There simply aren't enough letters actually making the sound that they should for learners to figure them out.

OFF TO JAIL

could
would
should
there
their
where
said
eight
through
– etc. –

These outlaw words are examples of having too few letters actually doing what they should so that we can read them. Readers will be unable to decode them, making them not figure-out-able. Your only bet is to send them to word jail and memorize them.

REHABILITATE MINOR OFFENDERS

These are the words that I like to refer to as completely figure-out-able. Although these words don't exactly do what they should, they aren't necessarily causing a great deal of trouble, either. In other words, using the SECRETS helps us get close enough to figuring them out and they pose no real threat to our overall effectiveness as readers and writers. So how can you tell for sure if a word belongs in word jail? If you teach preK through first grade, ask yourself if it can be read. For second grade and up, ask if your kids can spell it. This entitles them to get out of jail free.

(See the "SIGHT WORD TRICK" box on page 62. to see how easy it is to rehabilitate "minor-offenders" like: *what, of, was, some, love, from, come, want, above, etc...*)

NO JAIL TIME

> father
> mother
> brother
> comfort
> water
> about
> – etc. –

Are these words figure-out-able? Absolutely! Because learners will have enough skills (like the *th* and *er* SECRETS in the word *father*) to accurately attack most parts of the word, they are capable of getting close enough to the sound of the word to figure it out. Should they have any difficulty, just remind them to bend the vowel, and then ask "What word does it sound like?"

NO JAIL TIME

> the
> we
> me
> he
> she
> be
> – etc. –

Once learners know the SECRETS, most high-frequency words pose little problem and can be successfully sounded it out. As for the MOMMY E® not doing her job, this is true also, but she is doing the next best thing, which is saying *her* name. Think back to that hierarchy of likelihood of the most likely things to try when a word is not sounding out. First, check the vowels because they are the best place to start fiddling. Remember, SUPERHERO VOWELS® can either put their muscle arms up and say their names (long sound) or put on their short and lazy disguise (short sound). Try one, and then if that doesn't work try the other. See? It's really not so hard. I mean, it's not like MOMMY E® sounds like a *k*!

Voiced or Unvoiced *th*

I'm often asked about the voiced and unvoiced *th* sounds, and how students can discern which one to make when attempting to sound out words. The voiced *th* sound has vocal resonance, or vibration, due to engagement of the vocal cords (e.g., *the, them, those, etc.*), whereas the unvoiced *th* sound is made with the breath only, and has no vibration (e.g., *both, with, tooth, etc.*). Either sound (voiced or unvoiced) should get learners close enough so as to be able to recognize the word—making it figure-out-able! And this alone is our goal.

Another common question about the word *the* is in regard to the two ways it may be pronounced: one with a long *e*, and the other with the schwa (short *u*) sound. I am often asked, "So how will learners know which sounds to make?" The answer is just as before, "It doesn't matter." Getting the word is what matters, and from that point learners may pronounce it any way they please. It makes no difference to them that this word has two different pronunciations because once it has already been successfully sounded out, it may then be pronounced however they so choose. Again, it has no bearing on their ability to have successfully decoded the word in the first place. The learner simply tried both sounds possible for *e* and realized that long *e* was the correct sound, and thus got the word.

Remember, we aren't trying to be phonics specialists. Our number one priority is to focus on reading for meaning, continuing to build up that all important base of experience with text because that is how we will truly progress the most as readers and writers! So, for all other potential *th* offenders still out there roaming the text (both the voiced and unvoiced alike), this minor offense will not land you in jail because in the scheme of our language we simply have bigger fish to fry.

NO JAIL TIME

> **most**
> **old**
> **bank**
> **find**
> **child**
> – etc. –

These words have no MOMMY E® or BABYSITTER VOWELS® to make the vowels put their muscle arms up and say their names. However, once you start fiddling with the vowels a bit they become completely figure-out-able, as they still make their next most likely (short) sounds.

NO JAIL TIME

> **give**
> **have**
> **chance**
> **active**
> **since**
> **because**
> – etc. –

These words really aren't so bad and can definitely be rehabilitated. It just has a MOMMY E® who's not doing her job, but she isn't really causing any commotion, either. Everything else is figure-out-able as usual, so no real problem here.

NO JAIL TIME

> **pitch**
> **catch**
> **crutch**
> **castle**
> **wrestle**
> – etc. –

Even if learners include the *t* sound (which is silent) when sounding out these words, the extra sound will not impede their ability to hear— and thus figure out— the words.

The bottom line is that if we use SECRET STORIES® to get us close enough to actually read the word, then there's no need to memorize it (send it to jail) even if it is an exception.

Increased Brain Activity

Stanford University Professor Bruce McCandliss found that beginning readers who focus on letter-sound relationships, or phonics, instead of trying to learn whole words, increase activity in the area of their brains best wired for reading, according to new Stanford research investigating how the brain responds to different types of reading instruction.

"This is the first evidence that a specific teaching strategy for reading has direct neural impact. In other words, to develop reading skills, teaching students to sound out 'C-A-T' sparks more optimal brain circuitry than instructing them to memorize the word *cat*. And, the study found that these teaching-induced differences show up even on future encounters with the word."

This research sums up perfectly why we, as teachers, should focus our efforts on creating word *doctors*, as opposed to word *wardens*! Putting words in jail should be done only as a last result, and not simply because a word "breaks a rule" or doesn't follow a SECRET.

Evidence Base

SCIENCE OF READING & THE BRAIN

Dehaene, S. (2010). *Reading and the brain: the new science of how we read.* NY: Penguin Books.

Eide, B.L., Eide, F.F. (2012). *The dyslexic advantage: unlocking the hidden potential of the dyslexic brain.* NY: Plume Pub.

Gentry, R. J., Ouelette, G. (2019). *Brain words: how the science of reading informs teaching.* NY: Stenhouse.

Huttenlocher, P. (2003). *Neural plasticity.* Cambridge, MA: Harvard University.

Hirsch-Pasek, K., Eyer, D., & Golinkoff, R.M. (2003). *Einstein never used flash cards: how our children really learn— and why they need to play more and memorize less.* Emmaus, PA: Rodale Press.

Kosick, Kenneth M.D. (2008). *Rewiring the brain to improve learning.* Needham, MA: Public Information Resources.

Petty, G. (2014). *Evidence-based teaching- a practical approach.* Oxford: Oxford Press.

Pinker, S. (2015). *How the mind works.* London: Penguin Books.

Posner, M.I., & Abdullaev, Y.G. (1999). Neuroanatomy, circuitry, and plasticity of word reading. *Neuroreport 10*(9), 3.

Seidenberg, M. (2017). *Language at the speed of sight.* NY: Basics

Sousa, D.A. (2016) *How the brain learns.* NY: Corwin.

Shaywitz, S. (2005). *Overcoming dyslexia.* NY: Vintage Pub.

Sprenger, M.B. (2013) *Wiring the brain for reading: brain based strategies for teaching literacy.* NY: Jossey Bass.

Stanford University (2015). Reading: brain waves study shows how different teaching methods affect reading development. *Science Daily.*

Williams, R. (2017). Processing information with the non-conscious mind. *Journal Psyche.*

Willis, J. (2008). *Teaching the brain to read: strategies for improving fluency, vocabulary and comprehension.* VA: Association for Supervision & Curriculum Development.

Wolf, M. (2008). *Proust and squid: the story and science of the reading brain.* New York: Harper Perennial.

Wong, M. (2015). Brain wave study shows how different teaching methods affect reading development. *Medical Xpress.*

Zull, J.E. (2011). *From brain to mind: using neuroscience to guide change in education.* VA: Stylus Pub.

LITERACY INSTRUCTION

Adams, M.J. (1990). *Beginning to read: thinking and learning about print.* Cambridge MA: MIT.

Allington, R. (2011). *What really matters for struggling readers: designing research-based programs.* NY: Pearson.

Beck, I.L., & Beck, M.E. (2013). *Making sense of phonics: The hows and whys (2nd ed.).* NY: Guilford Press.

Berninger, V.W., Wolf, B.J. (2015). *Dyslexia, dysgraphia, owl ld and dyscalculia: lessons from science and teaching.* NJ: Brookes Publishing.

Blevins, W. (2019). *A fresh look at phonics, grades k-2: common causes of failure and 7 ingredients for success.* NY: Corwin.

Blevins, W. (2016). Meeting the challenges of early literacy phonics instruction. *International Literacy Association Research Panel Brief.*

Ehri, L.C. (1992). *Reconceptualizing the development of sight word reading and its relationship to recoding.* In P.B. Gough, L.C. Ehri, & R. Treiman (Eds.), *Reading acquisition* (pp. 107–143). Hillsdale, NJ: Erlbaum.

Fountas, I. (2016). *Guided Reading, Second Edition: Responsive Teaching Across the Grade Levels.* NH: Heinemann.

Gough, P.B., Hoover, W.A. (1990). The simple view of reading. *Reading and Writing: An Interdisciplinary Journal. 127-160.*

Kilpatrick, D. (2015). *Essentials of assessing, preventing and overcoming reading difficulties.* NJ: John Wiley & Sons.

Levrag, A., Hulme, C. Melby-Levrag, M. (2017). *Unpicking the developmental relationship between oral language skills and reading comprehension: It's simple, but complex.*

Meeks, L., Stephenson, J., Kemp, C., Madelaine, A. (2016). How well prepared are pre-service teachers to teach early reading? A systematic review of the literature. *Australian Journal of Learning Difficulties.* 21(2), 69-98.

Moats, L.C. (2010). *Speech to print: language essentials for teachers (2nd edition).* MD: Brookes Publishing.

Moats, L.C. (2016). What teachers don't know and why they aren't learning it: addressing the need for content and pedagogy in teacher education. *Australian Journal of Learning Difficulties,* 19:2, 75-91.

Pressley, M. (2012). Effective beginning reading instruction.

Journal of Literacy Research, (34) 2, 165-188.

Shanahan, T., Shanahan, C. (2017). Disciplinary literacy: just the faqs. *Educational Leadership,* 74(5), 18-22.

Snow, P. (2015). The way we teach most children to read sets them up to fail. *The Conversation.*

LEARNING AND MEMORY

Asher, J. (2009). *Learning another language through actions.* CA: Sky Oak Productions.

Csikszentmihalyi, M. (2009). *Flow state—the optimal learning experience.* NY: Harper-Collins.

Fisher, D.B, Frey, N., Hattie, J., (2016). *Visible learning for literacy, Grades K-12: Implementing the Practices that Work Best to Accelerate Learning.* Cambridge Press: Cambridge.

Hattie, J. (2012). *Visible learning for teachers: Maximizing impact on learning.* New York, NY: Routledge.

Pace Marshall, S. (2006). *The radical new story of learning and schooling a call for leaders.* New York, NY: Jossey-Bass.

Speer, N.K., Reynolds, J.R., Swallow, K.M., Zacks, J.M. (2009). Reading stories activates neural representations of visual and motor experiences. *Psychological Science,* 20(8), 989

AFFECTIVE/ SOCIAL-EMOTIONAL LEARNING

Bechara, A., Damasio, H., Damsio, A. (2003) Role of the amygdala in decision-making *Acad Sci, 985,* 356–69.

Bechara, A., Damasio, H., & Demasio, A. (2000). Emotion, decision making and the orbitofrontal cortex. *Cerebral*

Cortex, 10, 295–307.

Cahill, L., Prins, B., Weber, M., & McGaugh, J. (1994). Adrenergic activation and memory for emotional events. *Nature, 371*(6499), 702–4.

Davidson, R. (2003). Affective neuroscience and psychophysiology. *Psychophysiology, 40*(5), 655–65.

Fischer, K.W., Bernstien, J.H., Immordino-Yang, M.H. (2012). *Mind, brain and education in reading disorders.* Cambridge: Cambridge University Press.

Immordino-Yang, M. H. (2016). *Emotions, learning and the brain: exploring the educational implications of affective neuroscience.* New York: WW Norton & Company.

Immordino-Yang, M. H., & Damasio, A. (2007). We feel, therefore we learn: relevance of affective and social neuroscience to education. *Mind, Brain and Education.*

Moss, H., & Damasio, A. (2001). Emotion, cognition, and the human brain. *Academy of Science, 935*, 98–100.

ACTION-BASED/ KINESTHETIC LEARNING

Asher, J.J. (2012). *Learning another language through actions.* CA: Sky Oaks Productions.

Bjorkland, D., & Brown, R. (1998). Physical play and cognitive development: integrating activity, cognition, and education. *Child Development, 69*(3), 604–6.

Jeannerod, M. (1997). *The cognitive neuroscience of action.* Cambridge, MA: Blackwell Publishers.

Krakauer, J.W., Shadmehr, R. (2006) Consolidation of motor memory. *Trends in Neurosciences, 29,* 58-64

Wang, M.C., Walberg, H.J. (2004) *Building academic success on social emotional learning:.* NY: Teachers College Press.

AUDITORY LEARNING/ MUSIC

Aslin, R., Hunt. R. (2001). *Development, plasticity and learning in the auditory system.* Cambridge: MIT Press.

Carmichael, K and Atchinson, D. (1997). Music and play therapy: playing my feelings. *International Journal of Play Therapy, 6,* 63–72.

Chan, A., Ho, Y., & Cheung, M. (1998). Music training improves verbal memory. *Nature, 396,* 128.

Gordon, R.L., Fehd, H.M., McCandliss, B.D. (2015). Does Music Training Enhance Literacy Skills? A meta-analysis. *Frontiers in Psychology.* 6-19778.

Patel, D. Aniruddh. (2007). *Music, language & brain. NY: Oxford*

VISUAL LEARNING

Barton, R.A. (2005). Red enhances human performance in contests. *Nature, 435,* 293.

Kuhbandner C., & Pekrun R. (2013). Joint effects of emotion and color on memory. *Emotion, 13*(3), 375–9.

Kuhbandner C., Spitzer B., Lichtenfeld S., & Pekrun R. (2015); Differential binding of colors to objects in memory: red & yellow stick better than blue & green. *Front Psychology.*

Mehta, R., & Zhy, R. (2009). Blue or red? exploring the effect of color on cognitive task performances. *Science, (323)*5918

Martinez, J., Oberle, C., & Thompson, J. (2010). Effects of color on memory encoding and retrieval in the classroom. *American Journal of Psychological Research, Volume 6*(1).

NOTE: To access all of the musical tracks, use the download code found on the inside back cover.

Musical Brain Teasers

The musical brain teasers contained in the download are most effective when used in a spontaneous fashion during snippets of downtime found throughout the instructional day (waiting for the music teacher, standing in the lunch line, waiting for dismissal, etc…) The goal is to mix things up by plugging in different letters, sounds, and patterns, so as to constantly alter how each is sung.

TRACK 1: "THE 'BETTER' ALPHABET™ SONG"

Sing this song twice a day, every day, for two weeks to two months (this time frame applies to both preK and kindergarten students). It allows learners' muscle-memory to quickly acquire all of the individual letters and sounds (in the order of what's most likely).

Never The Same Way Twice!

Beyond the first five tracks, you will soon see that the musical brain teasers will almost never be sung the same way twice. They are ***never*** to be sung repetitively with no thought required, but used as a creative outlet for interactive manipulation and deeper ownership of the skills. They will mimic decoding and encoding processes when used in this way.

NOTE: To access all of the musical tracks, use the download code found on the inside back cover.

SCHWA SOUND

A slight shadow schwa ("uh" sound) can be heard following some consonant sounds, when sung. While minimized, its inclusion is intentional and for the purpose of more fully engaging learners' muscle memory as the primary means of sound-skill retrieval (see pgs 36-37). Additionally, current research shows that cutting-off this naturally occurring sound entirely can interfere with beginning readers' ability to blend when sounding out words. It is, however, best to minimize this sound so that it is not perceived as an additional sound when learners try to read or spell words.

TRACK 1: THE "BETTER" ALPHABET™ SONG
(tune of "Row, Row, Row Your Boat")

Sing letter sounds below	(they sound like)
A says a-a-a-a-a-a-a-a	apple
But it can also say a-a-a-a-a-a-a-a-a	apron
B says b-b-b-b-b-b-b-b	
C says c-c-c-c-c-c-c-c	cat
But it can also say s-s-s-s-s-s-s-s	circus
D says d-d-d-d-d-d-d-d-d	
E says eh-eh-eh-eh-eh-eh-eh-	egg
But it can also say e-e-e-e-e-e-e-e-e	even
F says f-f-f-f-f-f-f-f	
G says g-g-g-g-g-g-g-g	goat
But it can also say j-j-j-j-j-j-j-j	giraffe
H says h-h-h-h-h-h-h-h	
I says ih-ih-ih-ih-ih-ih-ih-ih	igloo
I can also say i-i-i-i-i-i-i-i-i	ice
J says j-j-j-j-j-j-j-j	
K says k-k-k-k-k-k-k-k-k	
L says l-l-l-l-l-l-l-l	
M says m-m-m-m-m-m-m-m	
N says n-n-n-n-n-n-n-n	
O says ah-ah-ah-ah-ah-ah-ah-ah	often
But it can also say oh-oh-oh-oh-oh-oh-oh-oh	over
P says p-p-p-p-p-p-p-p	
QU says qu-qu-qu-qu-qu-qu-qu-qu	quack
R says r-r-r-r-r-r-r-r	
S says s-s-s-s-s-s-s-s	
T says t-t-t-t-t-t-t-t	
U says uh-uh-uh-uh-uh-uh-uh-uh	umbrella
But it can also say u-u-u-u-u-u-u-u	unicorn
V says v-v-v-v-v-v-v-v	
W says w-w-w-w-w-w-w-w	
X says ks-ks-ks-ks-ks-ks-ks-ks	box
Y says y-y-y-y-y-y-y-y	yellow
But it can also say E or I, E or I or E	even / ice
And Z says z-z-z-z-z-z-z-z	

NOTE: To access all of the musical tracks, use the download code found on the inside back cover.

TRACKS 2–5: THE LETTER RUNS
(tune of "The Alphabet Song," aka "Twinkle, Twinkle Little Star")

Sing letter sounds

A B C D E F G
H I J K L M N O P
Q R S
T U V
W X Y
Z Z Z Z Z Z

> *Track 2—SHORT vowel sounds (slow version)*
>
> *Track 3—SHORT Vowel sounds (fast version)*
>
> *Track 4—LONG Vowel sounds (slow version)*
>
> *Track 5—LONG vowel sounds (fast version)*

MUSCLE ARMS

Remember, muscle arms *up* for the long sounds of the SUPERHERO VOWELS® and be sure to use the action cues when making their short and lazy, in-disguise sounds!

Song Instructions And Notes

The goal of these four tracks is solely to increase learners' level of skill automaticity, so as to instantly identify the most likely sound for each letter. These tracks mimic what learners must do when attempting to decode a word, which is to attack each letter with its most likely sound. "The Letter Runs" can be sung fast or slow, and with short vowel sounds or long, or even mixing it up and switching from long to short half way through! And for an extra challenge, try singing them to other tunes, like "Happy Birthday," or the "Star-Spangled Banner." You can even try singing them backwards! Unlike "The 'Better' Alphabet™ Song," these tracks move too fast to sing more than one sound for each letter, so for those letters that make more than just one sound (c, g, and y) you will only sing the one that's most common (g as in go, c as in car and y as in yo-yo) .

NOTE: To access all of the musical tracks, use the download code found on the inside back cover.

TRACKS 6–9: OLD MACDONALD
(tune of "Old MacDonald had a Farm")

REMINDER

Consonant practice with all letters except *a, e, i, o,* and *u.*

Track 6: Consonant practice
Examples: t, j, z

Old MacDonald had a farm,
e-i-e-i-o!
And on that farm he had a *t*,
e-i-e-i-o!
With a *t-t* here, And a *t-t* there,
Here a *t*, There a *t*,
Everywhere a *t-t*!
Old MacDonald had a farm,
e-i-e-i-o!

REMINDER

Short and long vowel practice for all five vowels.

Track 7: Vowel practice
short a, long e, long u

Old MacDonald had a farm,
e-i-e-i-o!
And on that farm he had a short *a*,
e-i-e-i-o!
With an *a-a* here, And an *a-a* there,
Here an *a* There an *a*,
Everywhere an *a-a*!
Old MacDonald had a farm,
e-i-e-i-o!

Track 8: Consonant blend practice
sl, tr, sw

Old MacDonald had a farm,
e-i-e-i-o!
And on that farm he had a *sl*,
e-i-e-i-o!
With a *sl-sl* here, And a *sl-sl* there,
Here a *sl*, There a *sl*,
Everywhere a *sl-sl*!
Old MacDonald had a farm,
e-i-e-i-o!

NOTE: To access all of the musical tracks, use the download code found on the inside back cover.

Track 9: SECRET STORIES® combinations   *ow, ar*

Old MacDonald had a farm,
e-i-e-i-o!
And on that farm he had an *ow*,
e-i-e-i-o!
With an *ow-ow* here, And an *ow-ow* there,
Here an *ow-ow* There an *ow-ow*,
Everywhere an *ow-ow*!
Old MacDonald had a farm,
e-i-e-i-o!

TRACKS 10–13: WHERE IS...?
(tune of "Where Is Thumbkin?")

Track 10: Consonant practice   *Examples: p, f, x*

Teacher: Where is *p*? Where is *p*?
Student: Here I am! Here I am! *p-p-p-p-p-p*!
Entire Class: *p-p-p-p-p-p! p* says, *p* says!

Track 11: Vowel practice   *long i, long o, short u*

Teacher: Where is *long i*? Where is *long i*?
Student: Here I am! Here I am! *i-i-i-i-i-i*
Entire Class: *i-i-i-i-i-i! long i* says, *long i*!

Track 12: Consonant blend practice   *bl, sp, pr*

Teacher: Where is *bl*? Where is *bl*?
Student: Here I am! Here I am! *bl-bl-bl-bl-bl-bl*
Entire Class: *bl-bl-bl-bl-bl-bl! bl* says, *bl* says!

Track 13: Consonant blend practice   *er, au, sh*

Teacher: Where is *er*? Where is *er*?
Student: Here I am! Here I am! *er-er-er-er-er-er*
Entire Class: *er-er-er-er-er-er! er* says, *er* says!

HAVE MORE FUN!

To make this one even more fun, give students hand-held manipulatives with the letters, blends and *SECRET STORIES®* to be sung, and have them stand and respond when they hear their sound!

NOTE: To access all of the musical tracks, use the download code found on the inside back cover.

TRACK 14: THE SUPERSONIC BLENDS
(tune of "Hokey-Pokey" with motions!)

VISUALS

Copy page 172 so you can cut apart the Blend Droplets for learners to use with the blender graphic when singing.

You put an *s* and *t* in,
You take an *s* and *t* out,
You put an *s* and *t* in,
And you shake them all about.
Turn on the phonic blender and you
blend them all about—
st, st, st, st, st, st

You put a *g* and *l* in,
You take a *g* and *l* out,
You put a *g* and *l* in,
And you shake them all about.
Turn on the phonic blender and you
blend them all about—
gl, gl, gl, gl, gl, gl

You put a *b* and *r* in
You take a *b* and *r* out
You put a *b* and *r* in,
And you shake them all about.
Turn on the phonic blender and you
blend them all about—
br, br, br, br, br, br, br

NOTE: To access all of the musical tracks, use the download code found on the inside back cover.

TRACK 15: THE BEETHOVEN BLENDS
(sung to the first four notes of Beethoven's famous Fifth Symphony)

Teacher (blend sound only!)	Students (letter names only!)
cl-cl-cl-cl	*c-l*
tr-tr-tr-tr	*t-r*
sl-sl-sl-sl	*s-l*
pr-pr-pr-pr	*p-r*
sp-sp-sp-sp	*s-p*
gl-gl-gl-gl	*g-l*
e-e-e-e-e	*long e*
ow-ow-ow-ow	*o-u / ow*
ch-ch-ch-ch	*c-h*

Song Instructions And Notes

The teacher sings the sound(s) of the letter(s), while learners respond with the letter name(s) that make the sound. Repeat this activity to practice identifying all blends, vowels (both short and long) as well as all of the SECRET STORIES® sounds. The next three tracks follow this same pattern, but in reverse (teacher sings letter name(s) and students sing the sound(s) of the letter(s).

I strongly suggest you practice this track, along with its reverse (Tracks 16–18) in conjunction with one another. Each provides the children with different opportunities, either to manipulate newly acquired skills or sharpen existing ones.

This musical brain teaser may also be used to practice both long and short vowel sounds, as well as SECRET STORIES® sound patterns. Jewelry Assessment Tools may be used for visual cuing of letters/patterns (see page 38, "Blend Bracelets And SECRET STORIES® Necklaces").

NOTE: To access all of the musical tracks, use the download code found on the inside back cover.

INSTRUCTIONS

Teacher sings letters and students sing their sounds. Students may need visual cues (such as pointing) to prompt their singing response. Jewelry Assessment Tools (pg. 38) may be used here as well as in the last track.

TRACKS 16–18:
BEETHOVEN BLENDS "IN REVERSE"
(sung to the first three notes of "Three Blind Mice")

Track 16: Blend letter prompt *Examples: cl, tr, sl, pr, sp, gl*

Teacher (letter names only!)	Students (blend sound only!)
c-l says	*cl*
t-r says	*tr*

Track 17: Consonant blends/Vowel practice
c-l short a, t-r long u, s-l short o, p-r long a, s-p long i, g-l short e

Teacher (sound only!)	Students (letter names only!)
c-l-short a	*cla (apple)*
c-l-long a	*cla (apron)*

Track 18: Consonant blends/SECRET STORIES®
c-l ou, t-r au, s-l ur, p-r ing, s-p or, g-l oa

Teacher (letter names only!)	Students (sound only!)
c-l-ou	*clou (*
c-l-au	*claw*

NOTE: To access all of the musical tracks, use the download code found on the inside back cover.

TRACKS 19–22: APPLES AND BANANAS— PLUS A LITTLE EXTRA!

(sung to the tune of "Apples and Bananas")

I like to eat, eat, eat, apples and bananas,
I like to eat, eat, eat, apples and bananas.

INSTRUCTIONS

For these four tracks the teacher will call out the letter name/names before the students sing the response. The teacher should not provide the sound at all– letter names only!

Track 19: Consonant practice   *Examples: t, r, z*

Teacher: *t*
Students: I like to teat, teat, teat, tapples and tananas,
              I like to teat, teat, teat, tapples and tananas.

Track 20: Consonant blends   *pr, sp, gl*

Teacher: *pr*
Students: I like to preat, preat, preat, prapples and prananas,
              I like to preat, preat, preat, prapples and pranaas.

Track 21: Blends/vowel practice
sm short i, cl long e, str short a

Teacher: *sm-short i*
Students: I like to smit, smit, smit, smipples and smininis,
              I like to smit, smit, smit, smipples and smininis.

Track 22: Consonant blends/SECRET STORIES®
spr-oo, sl-ir, th-ow, ch-ar, wh-ea

Teacher: *spr-oo*
Students: I like to sproot, sproot, sproot,
              sproopples and sproonoonoos,
              I like to sproot, sproot, sproot,
              sproopples and sproonoonoos.

4

SECRET STORIES®

Handouts
And
Cut-Apart Cards

Handouts For Copying

This section, along with the next two (Word Jail & Outlaw Mug Shot Cards and SECRET Skill Sheets), contain pages that may be reproduced for use with your class. These are the only three sections of this book that may be copied.

SUPERSONIC BLENDER

Make copies of this image on page 172 and allow your students to cut out the blend droplets. These make great manipulative practice, especially when you combine them with other letters and sounds so that they can make full words.

PARENT TEACHER LETTER

You may copy page 173 to send home with your students at the beginning of the year, or whenever you choose to adopt the *SECRET STORIES®* into your curriculum.

Dear Parents,

We use *Secret Stories*® in our classroom to help us figure out all of those tricky phonics sounds that letters make when they get together in words. Once we know all of the Secrets, we'll be able to read and write almost anything!

Don't be surprised when your child comes home talking about the strange behaviors of the letters! For example, did you know that the letters *au* and *aw* are in love? Yep, it's true! And they get so embarrassed when they have to stand together in words that they always blush and say, "*Awwwwwwww!*" (as in the words: *August*, *awful*, and *saw*). Or, that there are Superhero Vowels® with the power to say their names (though they have "short and lazy" disguises, as well!) There's also Mommy E® and the Babysitter Vowels®...... and even a Sneaky Y®! These simple stories make it easy for kids to remember all the crazy sounds that letters make when they get together, so that they can USE them for reading, writing and spelling!

Be sure to ask your child about the new Secrets they've learned, and if they have trouble reading or spelling a word, ask if they see (or hear) any Secrets in it!

For more information and for free parent resources to help support your child's independent reading and writing at home, go to **www.TheSecretStories.com/Learn-More/Free-Phonics-Resources-for-Parents**. You can also search for the "Secret Stories Phonics" App in Apple's App Store for more at-home reading and writing fun with the Secrets!

Word Jail & Outlaw Words Mug Shot Cards

Turn any bulletin board space into a word jail with some white paper backing and a black (or black and white) border. Make several copies of the larger mug shot cards and keep them nearby, ready to capture words as learners discover them throughout the day. (For more information on criteria for putting a word in jail see "Accepting Exceptions," pg. 137.)

For more individualized instruction, the smaller cards may be copied and provided to all students so that they may create their own, personalized word jails. This allows for easy differentiation of reading and/or spelling instruction.

Example of a word jail with outlaw word mug shot cards.

SECRET Skill Sheets

SECRET STORIES® are meant to be taught in context, which is the theme throughout this entire book. On the following pages you'll find SECRET Skill Sheets designed to provide targeted practice of specific patterns in text to systematically assess individual phonemic skill proficiency levels. In other words, you can use these sheets to see how well they use the SECRETS. Each one has a blank counterpart so that in addition to the random practice words I chose, you can have the students themselves look for words that use that particular SECRET. Do not have the students memorize the words on these sheets; instead encourage them to read using the SECRET they have learned.

Never Choose Skill Sheets Over Actual Text

Please keep in mind that working in context with whole texts is more important than working with these skill sheets. These sheets provide a great assessment tool, but they are not more important than reading whole text, which is what gives learners the most important and meaningful experience. Therefore, please be sure to alternate your small, guided reading group time with literature-based reading activities and opportunities in addition to the SECRET Sheet assessment and practice. Please do not ever use skill sheets or other such practice pages in place of more meaningful, authentic reading experiences. Use them only to support a learners' reading skill level practice, as well as for your own informal assessment needs.

Short and Lazy a

cat   bad

sat   sad

hat   add

at   dad

ran   man

band can

and   ran

nap   bag

What other "Short and Lazy a" words do you know?

DATE(S):

NAME:

Short and Lazy e

red	bend
bed	sent
end	let
fell	set
tell	pet
pen	met
ten	kept
send	left

What other "Short and Lazy e" words do you know?

Short and Lazy i

it   did

sit   big

hit   milk

in   wind

win   skip

will   list

fill   lick

him   pick

DATE(S):

NAME:

What other "Short and Lazy i" words do you know?

Short and Lazy o

not	mop
hop	pop
top	ox
dot	fox
lot	box
hot	rock
dog	on
log	jog

What other "Short and Lazy o" words do you know?

Short and Lazy u

cut	hum
nut	buzz
sun	luck
run	buck
up	mud
pup	tub
bug	rub
mug	puff

What other "Short and Lazy u" words do you know?

Short and Lazy Mixed

cat	led
cut	fun
sit	man
hit	but
mop	mud
sat	met
big	top
dug	and

What other "Short and Lazy Mixed" words do you know?

DATE(S): _____

NAME: _____

Mommy e ®

date	rose
cute	bone
bite	gate
like	use
hope	time
hate	make
bike	ice
cake	nice

DATE(S):

NAME:

Blends

flip	drip	drop
stop	flag	flop
stick	slap	trip
trap	swim	spell
frog	spot	spit
grass	club	from
spin	flat	drum
black	glad	crust

What other "Blends" words do you know?

DATE(S):

NAME:

Short & Long Vowel Blends

plate   grade   print

clip   trick   pretend

frame   spill   stripe

stage   trunk   place

price   print   planet

grape   prize   glide

spit   dragon   brag

stripe   drive   dress

What other "Short & Long Vowel Blends" words do you know?

DATE(S):

NAME:

Sneaky y®

my	baby
sky	sticky
by	funny
July	sunny
lucky	candy
study	bunny
yucky	try
shy	family

DATE(S): _____

NAME: _____

Two Vowels Go-A-Walkin' …

beat   boat

meet   coat

read   seed

suit   seat

boat   main

cue   brain

bait   feather

hue   head

sweet   bread

DATE(S):   NAME:

ar

far	yard
car	art
hard	farm
park	arm
March	barn
cart	yarn
smart	part
large	garden

DATE(S):

NAME:

What other "al" words do you know?

al

ball always

call almost

hall also

tall mall

fall small

metal medal

pedal petal

DATE(S):

NAME:

www.TheSecretStories.com / Permission to duplicate for student use.

er / ir / ur

bird	person
girl	center
bird	jerk
curl	sir
swirl	sure
first	circus
turn	circle
germ	corner

DATE(S):

NAME:

What other "or" words do you know?

or

or	north
for	sort
horn	Oreo
torn	sore
corn	ignore
door	snore
floor	before
born	forest

DATE(S): _____

NAME: _____

What other "au / aw" words do you know?

au / aw

August draw

yawn jaw

awful law

awesome lawn

cause saw

because straw

faucet crawl

pause dawn

DATE(S):

NAME:

What other "ou / ow" words do you know?

ou / ow

how	hour	slow
now	around	blow
cow	hour	know
down	count	yellow
brown	about	row
town	south	low
mouth	cloud	though
sound	proud	dough

DATE(S):

NAME:

oi / oy

joy	coin
boy	join
soy	foil
toy	soil
enjoy	spoil
coin	choice
noise	avoid
destroy	point
oyster	moist

What other "oo" words do you know?

oo

hoot	food	hook
room	too	book
soon	boom	look
spoon	bloom	cook
zoo	tooth	wood
root	nook	book

DATE(S): _____

NAME: _____

What other "ay / ey" words do you know?

ay / ey

ay		ey
say		they
play		prey
lay		grey
way		hey
away		Sunday
always		Saturday
key		Tuesday
turkey		Monday

Introduce homonyms here (words with alternative meanings/spellings) and share ay versions of these words (pray, gray, hay).

DATE(S):

NAME:

What other "qu" words do you know?

qu

quack	question
queen	quote
quarter	square
quilt	quiz
quit	frequent
quiet	squeeze
quite	squeal

DATE(S):

NAME:

What other "ch" words do you know?

ch

chew	bunch
rich	choir
pinch	chill
church	school
much	cheap
chorus	stomach
lunch	Christmas
crunch	schedule

DATE(S):

NAME:

What other "sh" words do you know?

sh

show	fish
she	flash
shy	rash
sheep	wish
ship	shark
shop	cash
shot	shirt
shelf	shell
sheriff	brush

th

the	there
this	thunder
that	path
these	thick
those	Thursday
then	thousand
than	throat
they	gather
them	thirsty

DATE(S):

NAME:

What other "wh" words do you know?

wh

why	whine
when	whisker
what	while
where	whip
which	whale
wheel	white
whimper	whisk

DATE(S):

NAME:

kn / wr / mb / gn / rh

know	gnat
knew	gnaw
gnarl	wrote
rhyme	dumb
knife	rhinoceros
write	thumb
wrap	rhombus
written	crumb

DATE(S):

NAME:

What other "gh" words do you know?

gh

ghost	laugh
ghastly	cough
sight	tough
fight	rough
right	light
bright	fright
enough	night

www.TheSecretStories.com / Permission to duplicate for student use.

DATE(S):

NAME:

ing / ang / ong / ung &
ink / ank / onk / unk

What other "ing / ang / ong / ung" and "ink / ank / onk / unk" words do you know?

ring	strong
rink	honk
sang	sank
sank	sunk
song	hung
sung	hang
chunk	ringing
stung	donkey

DATE(S):

NAME:

What other "ed" words do you know?

ed

played	locked
stayed	jumped
rained	looked
danced	cooked
turned	poked
pointed	skipped
hunted	hoped
stranded	hopped
waited	missed
decorated	wrecked

DATE(S):

NAME:

tion / ation / sion

question	station
election	equation
lotion	transportation
motion	evaporation
tradition	condensation
definition	tension
reflection	vision
addition	division
subtraction	revision

What other "tion / ation / sion" words do you know?

/

DATE(S):   NAME:

What other "ion" words do you know?

ion

onion

million

stallion

pavilion

bunion

DATE(S):

NAME:

i Tries e On For Size

What other "i Tries e On for Size" words do you know?

medium

immediate

curious

stadium

aquarium

serious

helium

auditorium

DATE(S):

NAME:

What other "ous" words do you know?

ous

joyous

famous

ridiculous

dangerous

generous

glorious

curious

serious

delicious

i trying e
on for size!

DATE(S):

NAME:

What other "ie" words do you know?

ie

cookie   grief

parties   brief

pennies   achieve

families   relief

babies   niece

stories   piece

field   believe

ce / ci / cy &
ge / gi / gy

cent	juicy
center	pencil
place	gentle
force	giraffe
city	age
citizen	gel
principal	generous
bicycle	circle
ace	gym

DATE(S):

NAME:

Babysitter Vowels®

motor	deny
making	remove
biking	lady
student	hibernate
icicle	writing
unit	baking
biting	shaking
photo	tiny
native	joking
baby	music

DATE(S):

NAME:

eu / ew

few   feud

new   neutral

knew   neuron

dew   Europe

blew

DATE(S): _____

NAME: _____

Mini Visuals: Cut-Apart Cards

SECRET STORIES® *Cut-Apart Cards* contained on the following pages are intended for small group reference only.

They may not be copied for any purpose, including distribution to students for individualized use in the classroom or at home. For these purposes, SECRET STORIES® *Porta-Pics* (sold in class sets of 25) are available and provide the ideal "portable" skill reference for use, both in the classroom and at home.

The *Porta-Pics* may be found on the SECRET STORIES® website (www.TheSecretStories.com).

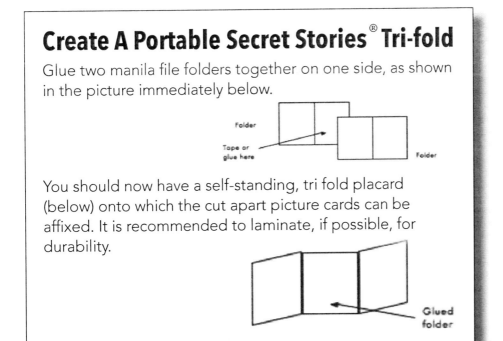

Create A Portable Secret Stories® Tri-fold

Glue two manila file folders together on one side, as shown in the picture immediately below.

Folder

Tape or glue here

Folder

You should now have a self-standing, tri fold placard (below) onto which the cut apart picture cards can be affixed. It is recommended to laminate, if possible, for durability.

Glued folder

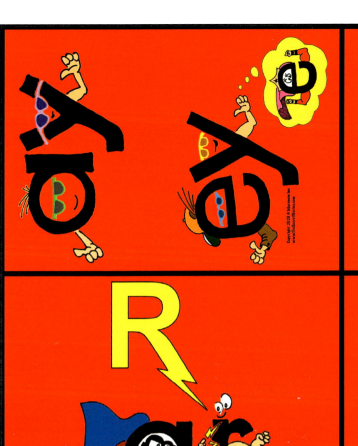

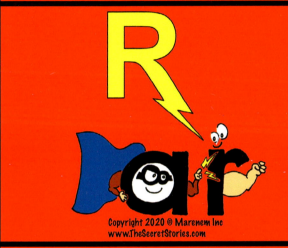

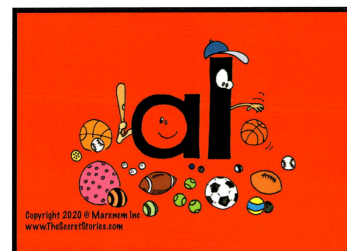

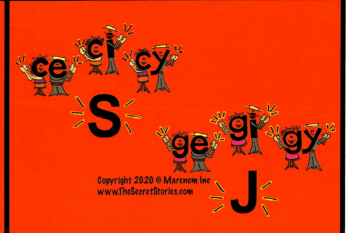

WORD JAIL

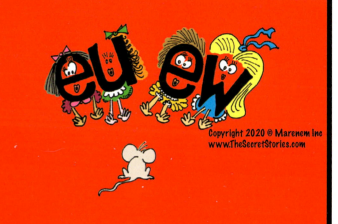

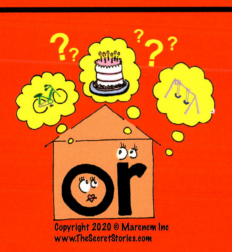

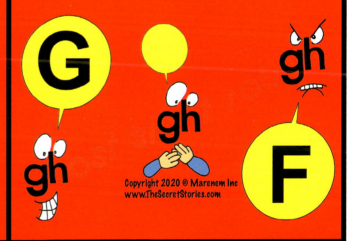

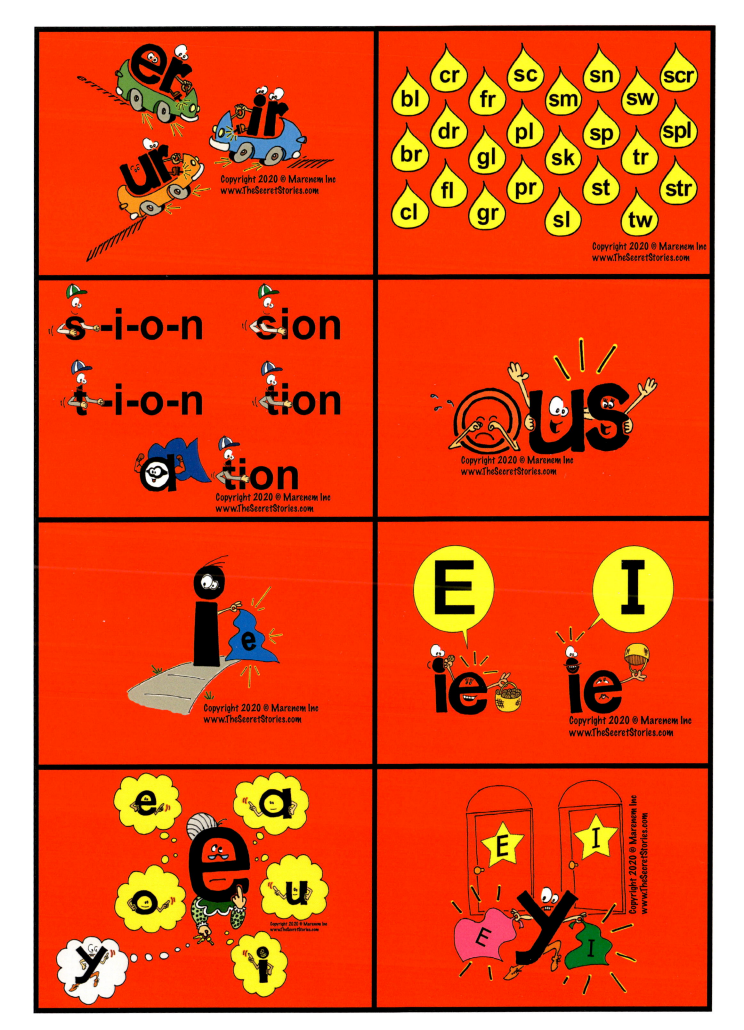